VIKINGS BEHAVING
REASONABLY

ARC IMPACT

Further Information and Publications

www.arc-humanities.org/series/book-series/

VIKINGS BEHAVING REASONABLY

NORDIC *HÓF* IN CIVIC AND LEGAL RHETORIC

by

ROBERT L. LIVELY

British Library Cataloguing in Publication Data

A catalogue record for this book is available from the British Library.

© **2024, Arc Humanities Press, Leeds**

ISBN (Hardback): 9781802700633
e-ISBN (PDF): 9781802702323

www.arc-humanities.org
Printed and bound in the UK (by CPI Group [UK] Ltd), USA (by Bookmasters), and elsewhere using print-on-demand technology.

CONTENTS

ILLUSTRATION

ACKNOWLEDGEMENTS

I WOULD LIKE to thank my mentors: Kathleen Lamp, Robert E. Bjork, and Peter Goggin. Their guidance and advice have helped more than they could ever know. I have been incredibly lucky to have such dedicated friends and mentors.

I would also like to thank the English Department and the Graduate College at Arizona State University, the English Department at Mesa Community College, Arnamagnæan Institute, the University of Copenhagen, the University of Iceland, and the English Department at Truckee Meadows Community College for their support in this endeavour.

During this project, I was afforded many opportunities to travel in Scandinavia. I would like to thank the endless numbers of guides, scholars, archaeologists, and friends who offered support and spent many hours with me as I researched this project.

Books are never a single author's endeavour. The Reference Librarians in the Elizabeth Sturm Library went out of their way to help with this book. Without the efforts of Jennie Allan, Maggie Eirenschmalz, and Laurel Harrison, this book could not have been completed. Dr. Jeff Alexander, Vice President of Academic Affairs at Truckee Meadows Community College and Dean Natalie Russell helped fund research, and LFT also provided additional funding for this project. Special thanks to Erek Lively for his suggestions during the writing process. I also want to thank Connie Skibinski, and Anna Henderson at ARC Humanities Press for their support and guidance through the publishing process. Additionally, I want to thank the anonymous reviewers who provided valuable feedback for revision.

Finally, I would like to thank my family, especially my wife, Shelby, for her love and support during this project.

Chapter 1

RHETORICAL CONTEXTS
IN VIKING STUDIES

The viking [*sic*] historian may equally fear that before he acquires all the
languages, reads all the books, and flushes all the coverts of all the peri-
odicals, he will have reached the blameless haven of senility without a word
rendered. Patently, to wait on definitive knowledge is to wait on eternity.[1]

THIS WARNING CAPTURES the problem with studying medieval Nordic
culture. The wide range of topics, geography, and languages is almost
paralyzing. Beyond the use of secondary sources, the scholar must also learn
the vernacular Old Norse in a variety of dialects, as well as a smattering
of runes and runic scripts. The wide swath of scholarship presents many
opportunities for research, but it also leaves just as many gaps. Medieval
Nordic studies rely on a variety of disciplines to create the mosaic of the
Viking north. Scholars use a variety of methods, including historical records,
runology, numismatics, saga studies, archaeology, manuscript studies,
folklore, and rhetorical studies, to create a better picture of the Viking Age.
Each field of study lays a tile in the mosaic—another place where scholars
can examine a facet of medieval Scandinavia. This book examines the civic
and legal rhetoric of the Viking Age in hopes of shedding light on the topic
from a rhetorical point of view, another angle of research, another tile laid.

One of the main problems in looking at the Viking Age is that its time
frames don't match well with traditional segments of medieval studies; but
grouping time frames with a moniker has always been problematic. The early
Middle Ages, or early medieval period, roughly 476–1000 CE, also overlaps
with the Late Antiquity running roughly from the 300s to 600s CE. The High
Middle Ages, or central medieval period, is classified as 1000 to roughly
1300 CE, and the Late Middle Ages ran from 1300 to ca. 1450 CE. But these
dates vary from place to place and sometimes scholars vehemently disagree.
Scandinavian cultural dates do not fit these eras well. Before the Viking Age,
the years from about 500 to 750 or 800 set the cultural foundation for the
Viking era. The Swedes call this the Vendel Age, but Norwegian and other
continental scholars often refer to it as the Merovingian Age, and it is also

---

1 Jones, *A History of the Vikings*, 11.

known as the Northern Germanic Iron age. To even further complicate matters, the Danes often refer to it as the Younger Germanic Iron Age. Whatever the name, this dynamic time period in cultural development set the stage for the Viking Age that followed.

Many scholars contend that the Viking Age starts at the first attack on the Lindisfarne monastery in 793 and lasts until Harald *harðráði* and the combined Norwegian, Northumbrian, and Orcadian army was defeated by the English ruler, Harold Godwinson, at Stamford Bridge in 1066. The Norse defeat at Stamford Bridge is often seen as a turning point since it stopped the Danish rule in England. But accounts of the defeat of Harold Godwinson by the Norman army just a few days later at Battle Hill, Hastings, fail to take into account that the Normans were themselves part Nordic, and that Harald *harðráði* and William the Conqueror were distantly related. This time frame takes an Anglo-centric view that the Viking Age started when they began bothering England and ended when they stopped. But the Scandinavians had extensive trade routes and still continued raids well after 1066. And the active range for the Scandinavian raids does not slot comfortably into standard periodization.

Judith Jesch argues that the Viking Age is much longer and more complex than that which I've just framed. Viking ships and their military tactics didn't spring into existence overnight before Lindisfarne, and their culture and raiding survived long after Harald's defeat at Stamford Bridge. Jesch points out that,

> Such dates are particularly favoured by historians, relying on specific events recorded in documentary sources…Beyond England, it is more difficult to pin down an exact date for the end of the Viking Age, especially if the conversion to Christianity is avoided as too imprecise or variable to be a marker…Military raids led by Scandinavian kings and chieftains continued well into the thirteenth century…The disappearance of the Scandinavian colony of Greenland at some time in the fifteenth century, the Scottification of the Northern Isles around the same time, and the Protestant Reformation throughout Scandinavia and its surviving colonies in the sixteenth century combine to suggest that c. 1500 is as good a date as any for the end of the 'long Viking Age.'[2]

These ideas of the diaspora and what constitutes the Viking Age are still debated by Scandinavian medievalists, but what is abundantly clear from the historical and archaeological evidence is the widespread colonization and influence on the medieval north by Scandinavian culture. There was

---

2 Jesch, *The Viking Diaspora*, 9–10.

enough consistency in language, people, and culture to name it a Viking Age. For the purposes of this book, I am taking Jesch's dates and suggesting the most active times of Scandinavian raiding and expansion took place between 750 and 1250 CE; by 1250 Christianity would have taken a stronger hold in Scandinavia, and the raids became less frequent outside of the immediate Baltic area. And the sagas by the Icelandic chieftain and priest Snorri Sturluson, which record this history, were composed in the early to mid-1200s.

The written records of the Icelandic people in the medieval period were the sagas, which recorded the life of the Scandinavians during the settlement and Nordic expansion periods, roughly 700 to about 1200. These sagas were written in the national vernacular, Old Norse, and were among the few Scandinavian records from that era. *The Grágás*, the Icelandic Law Code derived from earlier Norwegian law codes, was compiled during this time, and complements the sagas with the legal precedents of the day.

Many of the sagas were written in the 1200s to 1300s, and thus after the Christian conversion. However, the Nordic countries were converted rather late in European history (Denmark 826; Norway 995; Iceland 1000; and Sweden (officially) by 1130), and though it is tempting to associate the rhetoric in the sagas with the Christian Latinate rhetoric found on the continent, that is not the case. James J. Murphy's exploration of the topic was one of the major turning points in medieval rhetoric, and it lays out the three continental genera of rhetorical forms during the Middle Ages which are mostly lacking in the rhetorical forms in the north. Perhaps the only works that might apply as an *Ars poetriae* is the First Grammatical Treatise, a work on Old Icelandic phonology, contained in the *Codex Wormianus*, or Snorri's poetical tropes in the *Prose Edda*.

When Murphy's *Rhetoric in the Middle Ages* was published in 1974, it received mixed reviews. George Kennedy hailed Murphy's *Rhetoric in the Middle Ages* as "a significant contribution to the history of rhetoric in western Europe."[3] Kennedy points out the nuanced views of defining the three genera of Poetics, Letter Writing, and Preaching which form the preceptive tradition in the Latinate Middle Ages. While Kennedy views Murphy's bias against the sophistic tradition as unfortunate and potentially limiting, he does praise Murphy for contributing "a good perspective and values his subject. And he has clearly advanced the history of rhetoric a thousand years."[4] But Kennedy's optimistic perspective was not shared by all.

---

3 Kennedy, Review of *Rhetoric in the Middle Ages*,181.
4 Kennedy, Review of *Rhetoric in the Middle Ages*, 185.

John Norton-Smith's review of *Rhetoric in the Middle Ages* was scathing. He calls the work "dry and monotonous,"[5] and his disdain seems to stem from Murphy's synthesis of medieval texts to show that rhetoric was alive and well in the Middle Ages clinging to the textbook traditions of the surviving Roman books, particularly the *Rhetorica ad Herennium*, and other fragmentary Greek texts available to them. Norton-Smith dismisses Murphy's book in all areas except the chapter on the *Ars praedicandi* which Norton-Smith views as "profitably discussed."[6]

The most interesting aspect in these reviews is that Kennedy is a classicist who is interested in the history of rhetoric and translated Aristotle's *On Rhetoric* into English from the Ancient Greek, while John Norton-Smith is a literary critic and translator of medieval texts, mainly focusing on medieval England. Kennedy viewed Murphy's book as an advancement in rhetoric, Norton-Smith viewed it as a poorly written literary critique.

What Norton-Smith failed to see was that Murphy was attempting to show a continuity in rhetoric from classical times to the Renaissance. In his way, Murphy was countering the "rhetoric in decline" narrative. He was looking at the existing materials in the classical tradition and synthesizing them into a coherent thread of rhetorical practice. I agree with Kennedy that his work was groundbreaking at the time and did show rhetorical activity. But his scope was extremely limited to his three genera, *Ars poetriae*, *Ars dictaminis*, and *Ars praedicandi*.

The lens that Murphy uses shows the direct linkage to the classical tradition, especially in his discussion and analysis of the *Ars poetriae*. Murphy points out that Grammar is always the first of the liberal arts to be mentioned in medieval education. He argues that the modern reader often misinterprets the meaning of the word, "the term 'grammar' as commonly used today is severely narrowed...For us it merely denotes some standards of "correctness"...Early medieval grammarians made no such distinction. The *Ars grammatica* included not only correctness...but also the further study of what we would today call literature."[7] Murphy shows that the concerns of the Romans in linking style, grammar, and literature were still linked in the medieval period.

Drawing from the early medieval writers Donatus and Priscian, Murphy connects the idea of rhetoric back to the Roman schools and their use of literature in their curricula to develop style and better orators and writers. For

---

5 Norton-Smith, Review of *Rhetoric in the Middle Ages*, 327.

6 Norton-Smith, Review of *Rhetoric in the Middle Ages*, 326.

7 Murphy, *Rhetoric in the Middle Ages*, 136.

Murphy, the link from the Romans through the medieval period is unbroken in the teaching of rhetoric, from Cicero and Quintilian to such works as Priscian's *Praeexercitamina Prisciani Grammatici ex Hermogene versa* and *Institutiones Grammaticae*, Donatus's *Ars Minor*, to their influence on later writers Venerable Bede, Alcuin, John of Salisbury, and Geoffrey of Vinsauf. This connection to the classical world seems possible, and Murphy outlines the connections convincingly.

The *Ars dictaminis*, Murphy states, is a "truly medieval invention."[8] This invention has a long precursor before the medieval version of letter writing evolved to suit the needs of a feudal Europe. In antiquity, Murphy points out, there was evidence of oral transmission of messages as early as *The Iliad*. But this gave way to other forms such as *epistola*. Letters are regularly mentioned in the Bible and church uses. Pope Gregory the Great, for instance, was known for his letter writing skills. However, these letters had the problem of being rather formulaic. In the feudal era, the way to properly address various levels of society became formulae in which to compose. It eliminated the missteps of accounting for the level of the audience to whom you were writing.

Murphy argues the *Ars dictaminis* really started when Alberic of Montecassino developed the cursus or prose rhythm for composition of correspondence. As Murphy notes, "Alberic's major contribution to the *ars dictaminis* is his application of rhetorical principles to letter-writing."[9] Alberic uses *colores* (figures and tropes) and elements of his *Dictaminum radii* to expand the formulaic composition. Alberic looked at letter writing as a rhetorical exercise where he went from just thinking about figures to actually applying ideas of oral composition and the canon of rhetoric to the letter-writing process. In particular, "Alberic cites the Ciceronian objectives of the exordium, that is, to render the audience 'attentive, docile, and well-disposed.'"[10] Alberic's biggest contribution seems to take the writer from a place of passivity to one of agency, able to affect the reader of the letter.

Murphy's final section of rhetoric deals with the *Ars praedicandi*, the art of preaching. Murphy begins with the biblical origins and ideals of preaching and then ties in preaching to the larger Judeo-Christian context. Preaching was an early order of God, and to the early Christians, it was a religious duty. Murphy underscores that there was a major societal change here, where

---

8 Murphy, *Rhetoric in the Middle Ages*, 194.

9 Murphy, *Rhetoric in the Middle Ages*, 203.

10 Murphy, *Rhetoric in the Middle Ages*, 205.

"Neither Greek nor Roman civil society had a theocratic base,"[11] yet when monotheism became the cultural norm, the underpinning of civil society became a mix of civic and scriptural—a fundamental paradigm shift from earlier times.

According to Murphy, "Christ introduced a rhetorical element which had never before operated inhuman history—a direct command to his followers to spread his ideas through speech."[12] This edict led to the proselytizing mission of early Christians throughout Europe, Asia Minor, and Africa. The rhetoric of preaching changed the dynamic between speaker and audience. Where Ancient rhetoric often used speech as a means to influence the audience to the advantage of the speaker, Murphy claims St. Paul's tactic in preaching was a call to God. The preacher was a vessel for God's word, not a rhetorical orator seeking something for his own benefit. As Murphy explains it, the preacher lacks agency of his own because he is moved by God's will.

Perhaps the greatest book in antiquity on preaching is St. Augustine's *De Doctrina Christiana*. In this, Augustine reconciles a lot of rhetorical techniques with Christian theology. St. Augustine's contribution to saving Roman rhetoric is in his fourth book, where he gives "a defense of conventional Ciceronian rhetoric."[13] According to Murphy, Augustine ties rhetoric into one of the signs or manifestations of God where the rhetoric is a trigger to the way of God.

Rhetoric in the Middle Ages succeeded in showing that there were rhetorical practices in the Middle Ages. In that respect, Murphy's text opened new avenues at the time for further research; ironically, the problem arose where Murphy's three genera became fossilized as the *only* rhetoric to study in the Middle Ages. The intention of liberating scholars became one of limiting the research agenda into an ironically preceptive view of rhetorical study.

The rhetorical genres Medieval Europe adopted to make their society work are not found in the Icelandic Family Sagas. Nordic civic rhetoric relied on the citizens maintaining order in a decentralized society by means of reasonable action, and if their efforts didn't work, then they had recourse to a legal system built to reach reasonable outcomes. Their court cases didn't use elements of the Royal or Ecclesiastical courts, or the Classical Stasis Theory from Cicero to plead proceedings. The medieval Scandinavians had a different paradigm, based on their effort towards moderation and reasonableness. Analysis of the various scenes in the sagas show an importance in the

---

11 Murphy, *Rhetoric in the Middle Ages*, 273.

12 Murphy, *Rhetoric in the Middle Ages*, 273.

13 Murphy, *Rhetoric in the Middle Ages*, 286.

idea of reasonableness in the discourse conducted, and the overall approval of the people to men and women who practice a rhetoric of reasonableness. The Old Norse term, *hóf*, reasonableness or moderation, provides a framework for examining the civic and legal rhetoric of medieval Scandinavia. *Hóf* acts the way Gerard A. Hauser defines rhetorical functions.

> Rhetoric, as an area of study, is concerned with how humans use symbols, especially language, to reach agreement that permits coordinated effort of some sort. In its most basic form, rhetorical communication occurs whenever one person engages another in an exchange of symbols to accomplish some goal. It is not communication for communication's sake; rhetorical communication, at least implicitly and often explicitly, attempts to coordinate social action. For this reason, rhetorical communication always contains a pragmatic intent. Its goal is to influence human choices on specific matters that require attention, often immediately. Such communication is designated to achieve desired consequences in the relative short run. Finally, rhetoric is most intensely concerned with managing verbal symbols, whether spoken or written...*Rhetoric*, then, *is concerned with the use of symbols to induce social action.*[14]

Hauser lays out a definition that relies on social cooperation for the benefit of the group. This is exactly what *hóf* is designed to do. The various characters in the sagas are concerned with reaching agreements and keeping the peace while trying to uphold society's standards. This book seeks to expand that perspective to include how *hóf*, a rhetoric outside of Murphy's three genera, creates a framework to further broaden rhetorical research into medieval Scandinavian rhetorical culture.

---

14 Hauser, *Introduction to Rhetorical Theory*, 2–3. Emphasis in original.

Chapter 2

RHETORICALLY CONSTRUCTING
MEDIEVAL SCANDINAVIA

> Then the LORD said unto me, Out of the north an evil
> shall break forth upon all the inhabitants of the land."
>
> Jeremiah 1:14

WHEN THE VIKINGS first began plundering the English coastline in the late 700s, the monasteries along the coast provided rich and easy plunder for the sea raiders. The first major raid took place in England on June 8, 793 at Lindisfarne. The English monastery was thought to be secure from invasion. It was linked to the mainland by a narrow causeway which was underwater at high tide, so no invader could lay siege to the monastery. The rough waters of the North Atlantic at its back provided a natural wall from invasion. Inside the monastery lay treasures of precious metals, the beautiful Lindisfarne Gospels and the bones of St. Cuthbert. It was a seemingly invincible place to store sacred treasures of Christendom. When the Vikings approached by sea in their longships, the monks were unprepared for the onslaught. The Vikings came for treasure, and they took the gold and silver, sacked the altar, and took some of the monks as slaves. Since they weren't Christians, they didn't touch the gospel manuscript or the bones of Saint Cuthbert. For the Vikings, it was about plunder. To the Christians, it was an attack on a holy site. These seaborne attacks occurred on several monasteries over the next hundred years along the coasts.

The terrified monks kept records of the attacks and passed on letters giving biblical precedent on the evil of the north men. This Christian viewpoint helped to spread the reputation of the Viking warriors as not only a new point of conflict, but as a force of evil. After the attacks on Lindisfarne in 793, Simeon of Durham described the raid:

> And they came to the church of Lindisfarne, laid waste with grievous plun-
> dering, trampled holy places with polluted feet, dug up the altars, and seized
> all the treasures of the holy church. They killed some of the brothers; some
> they took away with them in fetters; many they drove out, naked and loaded
> with insults; and some they drowned in the sea.[1]

---

* A small portion of this chapter previously appeared in Lively, "We Must Always Go Fully Armed," 81–96.

[1] Qtd. in Magnusson, *Vikings*, 61.

This account of the raid travelled quickly to the court of Charlemagne in Aachen where the English monk Alcuin, who grew up near Lindisfarne, commented that,

> It is some 350 years that we and our forefathers have inhabited this lovely land, and never before in Britain has such a terror appeared as this we now have suffered at the hands of the heathen. Nor was it thought possible that such an inroad from the sea could be made.[2]

As the Viking attacks spread across Europe, the reputation of the Vikings as lawless killers cemented in the minds of the chroniclers of the day. Obviously, these accounts are from the point of view of the plundered rather than that of the raiders. Defining the Vikings through the writings of Christian Europeans has hindered full understanding of medieval Scandinavian culture for almost a thousand years.

In modern discourse, we tend to take a very reductive view of the Vikings. Many modern historians, for instance, focus on the brutality of the Viking raids, but many early cultures look extremely brutal by our contemporary standards. The Vikings were similar to the Romans, Saxons, Franks, Goths, or Celts in their tactics. Jonathan Clements comments on this tendency to stereotype Viking culture: "The Vikings were often defined by what they were not. They were, to the contemporary chroniclers that hated and feared them, *not* civilized, *not* local, and most importantly, *not* Christian."[3] But historians have mostly clung to the primary evidence written by survivors of raids against monasteries to paint the picture of the Vikings. In fact, many history texts focus mainly on Viking ships and military technology to capture the sense of the Viking Age.

Viewed as a counterpoint to this perception, the Icelandic sagas create a more complete picture of Nordic life and culture. These sagas show a complex people, and the sagas are known for being brutally honest in their rendition of life in Iceland.[4] The sagas offer an insider's view of the culture—an emic view. These sagas also show that the medieval Scandinavian people were extremely rhetorical in their thinking. The Norse used an organically constructed type of rhetoric, creating a rhetorical culture in their civic and legal practices. In this book, I argue that the major element of rhetorical practice employed by the Scandinavians in the Viking Age is a rhetoric of reasonableness (the Old Norse term, *hóf*). I argue that *hóf*, as a pervasive

---

2 Qtd in Jones, *A History of the Vikings*, 194–95.

3 Clements, *The Vikings*, emphasis in original, 12.

4 See Byock, *Medieval Iceland*, 36.

stance, permeated their rhetoric, and I work toward codifying its techniques and its transmission from generation to generation.[5] *Hóf* provided the Vikings with the functioning civic and legal rhetoric required to govern and keep the peace in medieval Nordic culture—a culture without strong central governments.

Delving into primary textual material in the sagas allows me to examine the rhetorical practices as recorded during the medieval period. The primary material provides clear evidence of rhetorical practices in the areas of governing and law, social rhetoric involved in maintaining a functioning society, and women's rhetorical practices delineating their rhetorical role in society. The sagas provide compelling evidence of insular medieval Nordic rhetorical practices which are seldom mentioned in historical texts but were obviously present.

The Myth of the Dark Age of Rhetoric

Along with the myth of the "Dark Ages" in history and literary narratives, rhetoric, too, seems to fall into a Dark Age from the ascension of Augustus to emperor of Rome to when the humanists began searching for ancient texts. The story of Poggio Bracciolini's discovery of Cicero's texts in 1415 at Cluny and his discovery of a complete text of Quintilian's *Institutio Oratoria* in the dusty stacks at St. Gall are legendary. In fact, according to Stephen Greenblatt, Bracciolini's find of Lucretius's poem *De Rerum Natura* in the Fulda Monastery in Germany sparked the Renaissance. Greenblatt's book, *The Swerve*, reinforces a narrative of the "Dark Age" when nothing important happened. His oversimplification of the medieval period ignores the rich and diverse cultures that arose after the fall of Rome. Greenblatt's contention that the modern world was spawned from a single rediscovery of Lucretius seems stretched, but it does easily fit into the popular narrative of the "Dark Ages."

The view of minimal rhetorical activity permeates medieval scholarship as well. Martin Camargo argues that rhetoric had "Little to no connection to vital civic life."[6] This narrative of decline is probably due in part to Kennedy's reasoning that the freedom necessary to have debates (and thus in his view, rhetorical activity) was reduced under Augustus and that freedom was lacking in Europe under the feudal system where feudalism and manorialism reduced freedom of the population even further. The hierarchical Mid-

---

5 See Kennedy, *Comparative Rhetoric*.

6 Camargo, "Rhetoric," 101.

dle Ages didn't seem to have a place for rhetoric. Brian Vickers's classic *In Defence of Rhetoric*'s chapter "Medieval Fragmentation" maintains this narrative. Vickers contends that rhetoric only works as "a discipline essential to the life of a democracy. When emperors or dictators rule, however, and such issues are decided by edict or by appointed administrators, rhetoric's role in society inevitably declines."[7]

A cursory view of the Latin West and Christianity in the Middle Ages would seem to support the narrative of a decline of the west followed by its salvation by the rise of Christianity, leading, in turn, to a rebirth of the Greek and Roman cultures led by humanists such as Poggio Bracciolini. Moreover, this narrative only works in the framework of the Greco-Roman tradition. Cultures outside this tradition engaged in rhetorical practices that have been marginalized by the canonical views of rhetoric. As Thomas P. Miller points out: "The Rhetorical Tradition is a fiction that has just about outlived its usefulness."[8] The Nordic peoples didn't live under emperors and dictators. They lived in isolated valleys and gathered in legislative assemblies across the Viking Diaspora. They were keen legal minds, and they developed a court system that worked for them. The rhetorical practices of the medieval Scandinavians were outside of the classical tradition, and they have been overlooked because they are not easily classified under the three genera—*ars poetriae, ars dictaminis*, and *ars praedicandi*—accepted by medieval scholarship.

Even as early as James J. Murphy's 1974 study, *Rhetoric in the Middle Ages*, he acknowledges that the conversation is incomplete "despite the apparently substantial number of authors and works treated in this book, this can only be a preliminary survey. Vast areas remain unexplored."[9] This becomes a common theme in well-known rhetorical studies, the acknowledgement of gaps and alternatives left unexplored. Bizzell and Herzberg echo Murphy's statement when they comment, "Given the state of scholarship at the time we assembled the first edition, it would have been very difficult to represent any alternative Western traditions, such as women's rhetorics or rhetorics of color."[10] But they do promise that these gaps will point to "future scholarship."[11]

---

7 Vickers, *In Defence of Rhetoric*, 214.

8 Miller, "Reinventing Rhetorical Traditions," 26.

9 Murphy, *Rhetoric in the Middle Ages*, ix.

10 Bizzell and Herzberg, *The Rhetorical Tradition*, v.

11 Bizzell and Herzberg, *The Rhetorical Tradition*, v.

Feminist rhetoricians offer ways to examine marginalized rhetorics. Cheryl Glenn argues that there were many women participating in rhetoric contemporaneously with the canon—yet were generally ignored by earlier scholars. As she points out,

> Fortunately, rhetorical scholars of every stripe are involved in various re-tellings and remappings of rhetorical history, all acknowledging the political nature of their work and the biases mined in their own rhetorical territory. In particular, the recent body of historiography in which feminist research-ers recover and recuperate women's contributions to the broad history of culture-making constitutes a new, more scenic excursion into the history of rhetoric.[12]

The new forms of rhetoric thus often ask for acknowledgement from the canonical scholars to establish their credibility, then create a new space to develop new research. Delving into medieval Scandinavian rhetoric, I kept Glenn's vision of making a more "scenic excursion" forefront in my mind.

Historical Investigations into the Vikings

When researchers consider the term "Dark Ages," they usually consider the time frame from the fall of Rome to around the beginnings of the Renaissance, or the rebirth of classical literature and culture, roughly from about 500 to 1400. The scholar William Patton Ker delineates the Dark Ages from about 500 until 1200, when he says the Middle Ages began. The Italian Humanist Petrarch coined the term "Dark Ages" to lament the fact that Latin language and literature was in decline, but his term was extended to mean a lack of cultural advancement in general after the fall of Rome. This perception of the Middle Ages upon non-medievalists has hindered the research and popular perception of the political, religious, and cultural advances which occurred during this timeframe. The idea of a "Dark Age" is popularized and spread through popular works such as Michael Wood's book and PBS documentary *In Search of the Dark Ages* and the History Channel documentaries in 2015 and 2017, lamenting the fact that the Dark Ages were times of plague, fam-ine, and internecine wars with little cultural advancement.

Unfortunately, both of the time frames listed above encompass the rise and fall of the Viking Age. Earlier historians and scholars may have viewed the Viking Age as uninteresting, since it wasn't until the late 1800s that scholars turned their attention to the medieval north and the Scandinavian people. This research manifested itself in archaeological finds in the 1850s

---

12 Glenn, *Classical Rhetoric Retold*. This extract is from the abstract.

of the Tune ship mound in Østfold, the excavation of the Gokstad ship in 1880, and the early 1904 excavation of the Oseberg ship. The Victorians, in particular, seemed to find the Vikings interesting, or at least curiosities. Since the Victorians revelled in curiosities and unusual artifacts, the sordid tales of Viking raids and plundering, for some reason, caught their attention, and scholars began researching the Vikings with renewed vigour.

The twentieth and twenty-first centuries saw the blossoming of medieval Nordic historical works. Perhaps the best known is Gwyn Jones's *A History of the Vikings* (1968). This important work offers a look into the early development, before the 700s, of the Nordic peoples who became the Vikings, and then explores the three major Nordic kingdoms of Denmark, Norway, and Sweden. Along with the obvious technological advances in ship building and seamanship, Jones traces overseas expansion to the Orkneys, the Faeroes, and Iceland. Moreover, he examines the mercantile efforts of Scandinavian traders on the continent and their ventures down the Volga to the Mediterranean cultures of the Islamic and Byzantine empires.

Jones seems truly impressed with the Viking culture of the north, and he traces the people and development of the three major northern kingdoms, but his work looks at the broad history of the Vikings. Even though he has many references to *þings* and the legislative and judicial functions they served, he never uses the terms rhetoric or rhetorical when discussing these activities. Jones is writing a sweeping history which follows major people and events, but he does not turn his gaze to the acts of rhetoric in shaping these events. Unfortunately, this becomes commonplace in examining the histories written about the Scandinavian people. Violence is an acceptable topic while the rhetoric of governing and legality is not considered.

Historians have continued to write about Vikings and the medieval north. Beyond Jones's *A History of the Vikings*, still a standard reference for Viking studies, recent scholarship seems to show a clear split in historical accounts of the medieval Scandinavians. Jesse Byock's work, for instance, attempts to show that the Vikings were much more complex than the typical barbarian portrayal commonly displayed in history books and popular culture. Using Iceland as his main area of research, Byock's work describes the Icelanders during the settling of Iceland in the 930s that "Iceland functioned as a single island-wide community or 'great village'. Inward-looking, highly litigious and hardly military, the new society operated through consensual order."[13] In a similar vein to Byock, William Ian Miller's *Bloodtaking and Peacemaking* (1990), explores the limited use of violence in Icelandic

---

13 Byock, *Viking Age Iceland*, 3.

society. Chapter 8 of Miller's work focuses on peacemaking, which was far more common than the negative views of Vikings would lead us to believe. "If peace means the absence of violence then peace was in fact the norm."[14] For the average Scandinavian, a peaceful life on a small farmstead was much more likely than a life of bloody raids and violence.

Similarly, in Anders Winroth's *Age of the Vikings* (2014), he focuses on the bits of culture that explore the day-to-day life and experiences of the Vikings. He introduces passages of colourful historical fiction into the book to better illustrate the history he is portraying. He goes out of his way to show that the medieval Scandinavians were more than just a stereotype of violence which is often shown by the Christian chroniclers.

> What is preserved is certainly only the tip of the iceberg, and much has been lost...Nonetheless, what survives of poetry, representational and decorative art, and stories teaches us that the Viking Age was not only about raiding, plunder, and warfare. Scandinavians had a sense of beauty and an ear for poetry, and they developed idiosyncratic styles of both art and literature without any close counterparts in the rest of Europe.[15]

On the other hand, some recent scholarship has pushed back against this more expanded view of Viking life. Jonathan Clements's *The Vikings: The Last Pagans or the First Modern Europeans* (2005), paints a somewhat mixed picture. He acknowledges their cultural complexity, but maintains that they needed to be tamed by land and Christianity before they could be considered cultured. Clements remarks "Take the Viking out of the longship, turn him into a farmer, and suddenly he worries about crops, disease, trade, and family. He welcomes law and order."[16] Although Clements fails to acknowledge that, in Scandinavia, the Viking was probably a farmer who *already* worried about these things, and who was *already* participating in law and order in his village, or on his farmstead, his work is a step toward a richer understanding.

However, this more nuanced understanding is not without its detractors. Robert Ferguson's 2010 study, for example, attempts to diminish the cultural complexities of the Viking culture. He downplays the Scandinavian scholarship into the nuances of the Viking Age by describing it as constructed "cultural identity,"[17] claiming that Scandinavian scholars are just

---

14 Miller, *Bloodtaking and Peacemaking*, 259.

15 Winroth, *The Age of the Vikings*, 240.

16 Clements, *The Vikings*, 80.

17 Ferguson, *The Vikings*, 5.

painting their forefathers as "noble savages."[18] Ferguson's thesis argues, "Among the aims of this book is to restore the violence of the Viking Age."[19] This historiographical point of view of the Vikings is perhaps best captured in the description of the Vikings, by David Dumville, as "long-haired tourists who roughed up the locals a bit."[20] Such reductive scholarship undermines the conversation of what the Viking Age was really like.

One of the more recent books on the Norse, Judith Jesch's *The Viking Diaspora* (2015), argues that the Viking Age is much harder to pin down. Jesch looks at historical, literary, and archaeological evidence to get a better sense of the Nordic peoples. She argues that the dates of ca. 750 to 1100 usually applied to the Viking Age are very problematic, since the Norse were active sea traders before this, and the Vikings didn't stop raiding after the loss at Stamford Bridge in 1066. Jesch points out that the chroniclers show active Viking Raids in the 1200s in the Mediterranean and into the 1300s in the Baltic Sea, and she argues that the Viking Age should be amended to include the final collapse of the colony in Greenland in the 1500s. At this point, the Scandinavians were no longer expanding their colonies—they were retreating back into Scandinavia or were permanently settled in other places. She coins the term "The Long Viking Age" to refer to this increase in timeframe.

Jesch argues quite convincingly that the diaspora includes periods of intense violence and raiding followed by times of peaceful trading and exploration. To characterize the Long Viking Age as inherently and continually violent is painting an incorrect picture of the Nordic peoples in that era. Jesch points directly to the Icelanders as "the most visible and lasting monuments to the Viking Diaspora."[21] She goes on to point out that "the diasporic consciousness of the medieval Icelanders" is "also an important interpreter of the Viking Age to subsequent generations."[22] The sagas and historical works by Icelanders, in her view, are among the best representations of the medieval diaspora captured for posterity.

Scandinavia was more complex than these renewed attempts to create a Nordic "Other" suggest. Rather than extending the conversation about the medieval Scandinavians, these violent histories offer outdated views of the medieval Scandinavians as war-like thugs. By our standards, most medieval

---

18 Ferguson, *The Vikings*, 5.

19 Ferguson, *The Vikings*, 6.

20 Qtd. in Ferguson, *The Vikings*, 9.

21 Jesch, *Viking Diaspora*, 199.

22 Jesch, *Viking Diaspora*, 199.

culture would be considered extremely violent, but by not focusing solely on that, scholars can attempt to explore and expand our knowledge of that era. Scholars such as Winroth, Jesch, and Byock suggest a more nuanced approach to studying the medieval Scandinavians. It is important to consider the histories to see the ideas of reasonableness in medieval Scandinavian culture. *Hóf* played an deeply important role, and it is in this spirit that I explore the rhetorical practices of the medieval Scandinavians. These people were demonized as heathen barbarians, and their rich culture often denigrated by chroniclers of the day. However, the tradition of the saga manuscripts, current historical work, and archaeological finds points to *hóf* as a major rhetorical *topos* across medieval Scandinavia.

Medieval Scandinavian Manuscripts

It is important to examine what we mean by texts in Old Norse. According to Matthew P. Driscoll, most texts from the medieval period are fragmentary. Fifty-one per cent of the corpus is made up of five leaves or fewer and 15 per cent of those are part or single leaves. The most common complete, or almost complete manuscripts, are copies of the originals, or copies of copies, from the fourteenth, fifteenth, or sixteenth centuries. He estimates we only have fragments of perhaps 7–15 per cent of the manuscripts that were composed in the Old Norse period.[23]

Textual scholars draw from a long tradition of textual editing, and textual criticism aims to restore texts as nearly as possible to their original form. This method of historical inquiry is about solving the problem of transferring a manuscript text preserved in script to a modern medium through which most of us work. We really accept, either implicitly or explicitly, that these textual critics have done their work accurately.

There are two main schools of thought in this: the Lachmann Method (or sometimes called Neo-Lachmann depending on the methodology used) and the Bédier school. The Lachmann Method arises from the German philologist Karl Lachmann (1793–1851). His method was described as a genealogical approach. He took a broad view of the surviving texts and tried to establish a history of the transmission of the text. His method creates a stemma codicum, which develops a tree-like structure showing the relationships between the main surviving texts of a work. By doing this, the method attempts to distinguish between later mistakes and additions to a text, and to determine which were artifacts from the earlier or original text.

---

23 Driscoll, "Introduction to Manuscript Studies."

This methodology is thus an attempt at reconstructing a text. This method examines texts and focuses on similarities and differences and often focuses on errors to establish the genealogy of a text. Lachmann's ideas on textual criticism and reconstruction were not new ideas. His methodology was pioneered by the School of Alexandria's methods of trying to reconstruct Homer's works which took an eclectic approach to constructing a manuscript to examine. Modern saga studies use a Neo-Lachmann Method which is more interdisciplinary. They use historical and archaeological data as well as computer modelling to reconstruct saga texts. I believe this method helps solidify their choices for the reconstructed texts since the triangulation of data with computer modelling gives the method a better chance of correctness.

The other method of constructing a text is from the Bédier school. Joseph Bédier (1864–1938) rejected the idea of the stemma codicum as being objectively scientific since it relies on data from scribal errors and linguistic similarity which cannot be one hundred per cent accurately studied. When building a stemma, researchers may find many versions are discarded as irrelevant since they are so close in construction. According to Bédier's theory, these reconstructed texts are more hypothesis than fact. So Bédier viewed the composite editions as not reconstructed originals, but as a completely new version that had never existed before. Instead, Bédier used a method that was originally pioneered in ancient Pergamon by Stoic editors who tried to find the "best text" available.

Bédier looked at all available texts to determine a best edition. He realized that this was a more subjective approach, but it is a more conservative attempt to present a medieval text as it was rather than building a new version based on all extant versions and scraps of texts. Both practices are used in Scandinavian manuscript studies. These historical reconstructions help scholars better understand and contextualize medieval Scandinavian culture.

Conclusion

Medieval Scandinavians suffered from the negative portrayals by the Christian chroniclers who viewed the pagan raiders as some sort of scourge of evil loosed upon the land. The attacks on Christendom seemed to portend an era of darkness and evil upon Europe. To the chroniclers, this seemed a reasonable assessment of what was happening. The Norsemen who came as raiders no doubt frightened the monks, who had felt safe in their secluded monasteries, nominally protected by Christian lords in a feudal system. The negative textual evidence about the Vikings attacks on these Christian holy places influenced the perceptions about medieval Scandinavians for a thousand years.

This perception also played into the creation of the myth of the "Dark Ages," a time of regression, violence, and stagnation. The "Dark Ages" narrative makes a false dichotomy between the light of Christianity and the sea of pagan darkness in Northern Europe. But this narrative works from a within a limited frame. From Britain and the Continent, it is an understandable point of view—an outsider's view of the north. However, the Scandinavians also wrote accounts of their world, in sagas and on runestones, which paints a different picture—one of a life in Scandinavia that functioned outside of European feudal models.

These sagas paint a picture of the lives, struggles, and successes of the medieval Scandinavians. The manuscript tradition in Scandinavia is a rich one, but the dearth of sources can sometimes hinder an attempt to describe their world. The Arnamagnæan Institute in Denmark and Iceland has worked to preserve these manuscripts and the textual tradition of the medieval north. These manuscripts describe the insiders' view of the culture as a more complex counterpoint to the chroniclers' less-than-flattering portrayal.

Chapter 3

GEOGRAPHY AND ITS
RHETORICAL IMPLICATIONS

One's Home is Best/Though hut it be:
There a man is master and lord;
Though but two goats thine/and a thatched roof,
'tis far better than beg.

Hávamál (Sayings of the High One)[1]

FROM THE AUSTERE shores of Norway to the rolling fields of Sweden, the impact of geography on the development of Scandinavian rhetoric cannot be overstated. Northern Europe's harsh climate meant that cooperation among its inhabitants was essential to survival. Lack of cooperation among the citizens of the clans and villages could foretell hardship and death for its people. Social structures were needed that did not rely on strong central governments. These structures relied on Scandinavian civic and legal rhetorics, at the core of which was *hóf*—the rhetoric of reasonableness.

The early classical influence that Christianity brought to the north, and to its rhetorical practices in particular, is largely lacking in Scandinavia. The impressive Swedish folklorist and scholar Ebbe Schön contends that Christianity's influence in medieval Scandinavia has been greatly overstated. Although many scholars contend that sagas and law codes written after the conversion are largely influenced by the new religion, Schön argues that Christianity was slow to take hold in the north. His work in Sweden suggests that in Lovön, an island near Stockholm, it took about 150–200 years for the population to become predominantly Christian.[2] Lovön is centrally located in the Swedish kingdom, so the hinterlands may have been even slower in their conversion. If Schön's argument is correct, then even if the sagas and law codes were written after the "conversion," they may only contain a glaze of Christianity. Kennedy's assessment of this phenomenon supports Schön's argument: "Classical rhetoric as understood in the early Middle Ages found a limited practical application in a number of oral and written forms."[3]

---

1 *The Poetic Edda*, trans. Hollander, 20.

2 See Schön, *Asa-Tors Hammare*.

3 Kennedy, *Classical Rhetoric*, 204

Outlying areas of Scandinavia may have experienced a slow spread of Christianity. Since many of the Nordic countries were converted later to Christianity only in the tenth and eleventh centuries, the impact of Christianity on the native rhetoric would have been minimal. Iceland, for instance, was considered the edge of the world, and Christianity may have spread even more slowly there. At the time Icelandic historians, Ari Thorgillsson and Snorri Sturluson, were writing, Christianity may not have influenced the writing as much as the modern reader may believe. If this is the case, then we must consider that all the trappings of Christianity, including their use of classical rhetoric, would also have taken a long time to permeate the culture, thus preserving many elements of the native rhetorical traditions.

Historically, the Northern Germanic peoples were known in antiquity. Several scholars have discussed the relationship between the runes and either the Roman or Etruscan alphabets.[4] The trade connections with the Mediterranean world clearly influenced the shape of letters in the runes used by the Scandinavians in their ubiquitous carvings. Additionally, early maps by Pytheas of Massalia (ca. 300 BCE) show the peninsula of Jutland and describes the lifestyle as agricultural and poor by his standards.[5] Orosius's *History Against the Pagans* describes an early Northern people, the Cimbri, who were often in conflict with Rome which Orosius paints in a biased way:

> The enemy [the Cimbri] captured both camps and acquired an enormous quantity of booty. In accordance with a strange and unusual vow, they set about destroying everything which they had taken...the horses themselves drowned in whirlpools, and men with nooses round their necks were hanged from trees. Thus there was no booty for the victors and no mercy for the vanquished.[6]

Tacitus, the Roman Senator and Historian writing in the first century CE describes the northern Germanic peoples in a very different light: "They [The Chauci] are the noblest peoples among the Germans and one that prefers to maintain its greatness by righteous dealing. Free from greed and from ungovernable passion, they live in peaceful seclusion; they provoke no

---

4 The Runic alphabet clearly shows a Mediterranean influence. Most Scholars view contact with Rome as the source of the similarity (see Tómasson, "History of Old Nordic Manuscripts I," 793–801, and Antonsen, "The Runes," 137–58). However, Gwynn Jones (*History of the Vikings*, 19–22) sees a possible earlier connection to the Etruscans. Richard Leo Enos ("Scriptura Etrusca," 36–61) argues more forcefully that the connection is actually to the Etruscan alphabet, since the Romans borrowed heavily from their Italic neighbours.

5 Jones, *History of the Vikings*, 21.

6 Qtd. in Jones, *History of the Vikings*, 21.

Viking Age trade routes in north-west Europe.
Map by Brianann MacAmhlaidh. Source: Wikimedia Commons.

wars and do not engage in raids for plunder."[7] Tacitus goes on to mention both the Swedes and the Dani (the Danes) as emerging into separate and competing kingdoms.

The point which emerges here is that the preserved historical records indicate that early on in northern history there were peoples who were known to be Scandinavian. They lived at the edge of the known world, were pagan, were a warrior society, and were different than the Germans whom the Celts and Romans had frequent contact. These small tribal kingdoms were often lumped together as Danes because these were the people inhabiting the Jutland peninsula and were often in the most contact with other

---

7 Tacitus, *Agricola and Germania*, 55.

cultures. Moreover, the Scandinavians were generally considered a single people because they spoke the *dönsk tunga* (lit. the Danish Tongue, but what we would consider Old Norse).

This interpretation of a single Danish people is somewhat misleading. Due to the nature of the small, isolated settlements of Scandinavia, there were many dialects and variations of language among the Nordic peoples. While it is true that variations of Old Norse were intelligible with each other, many dialectical variations existed, particularly the split between west and east Old Norse. However, to the outsider chronicling the Nordic peoples, these variations would have gone unnoticed.

The Viking raids are probably the most notably chronicled events from Scandinavia, but the Scandinavians were more often traders than raiders. The Nordic trade routes spanned the known world from Baghdad to the New World. The *Historiska Museet* in Stockholm, for example, displays many artifacts found in trade sites from as far away as China and Ireland. These artifacts testify to the widespread trade routes established during the Middle Ages; the perception of the Danes as violent interlopers is simply not correct.

Since there is evidence of a cultural unit of "Danes," the following regional accounts all belong to a single geographical span and related cultural unit.[8] Furthermore, this cohesive cultural unit is inherently important in showing the rhetorical stance of *hóf* as a value to the medieval Nordic peoples across the span of the north.

Pan-historiography challenges the current trend toward "more restricted or focused histories."[9] Hawhee and Olson see this research trend as hampering some fields because it fails to "explore the rhetorical histories of a concept or cultural group."[10] Their essay deals with the wider swaths of rhetorical history, while my research of *hóf* in medieval Nordic rhetoric only works as a broad look at culture. Since the people who spoke the Danish Tongue (i.e., the Scandinavians) had a similar language and cultural institutions across a large geography and time, and by focusing in at specific references from the sagas, I can make some guarded claims about the Nordic rhetorical culture.

As Hawhee and Olson note, "The decision to span depends upon and responds to the aspects of rhetorical history or theory that the study hopes to illuminate and the contributions a rhetorical perspective might make to

---

8 Hawhee and Olson, "Pan-Historiography," 90–105.

9 Hawhee and Olson, "Pan-Historiography," 90.

10 Hawhee and Olson, "Pan-Historiography, 90–91.

clarifying the broad themes."[11] Spanning is a very important concept for pan-historiography. Spanning both geographical area and time frames allowed me to show how the Nordic concept of *hóf* led to a stable social structure wherever the Norse settled over a span of almost five hundred years in the Viking Age.

Moreover, since "historiography always involves making selections. With more expansive histories, those selections slice up time, selecting representative figures or movements in order to create a larger narrative arc."[12] Spanning allowed me to demonstrate how broad frames of civic and legal culture are reinforced by specific instances in the histories and sagas of the Norse to build my case; thus, spanning both geography and time, and using both written and material artifacts, help expose the rhetorical practice of *hóf* that has been missing from rhetorical history of the medieval Nordic peoples.

Denmark

Due to their geographical connection to continental Europe, the Danish were in the most contact with Christianized Europe. Adam of Bremen's *History of the Archbishops of Hamburg-Bremen* describes the Danish lands like this:

> The principal part of Denmark (called Jutland) extends its lengthwise from the Eider River north; it is a journey of three days if you turn aside in the direction of the island of Fyn. But if you measure the distance direct from Schleswig to Alborg, it is a matter of five to seven days' travel...The soil in Jutland is sterile; Except for places close to a river, nearly everything looks like a desert: It is a salt land and a vast wildeness...Jutland itself is frightful in other respects. The land is avoided because of the scarcity of crops, and the sea because it is infested by pirates. Hardly cultivated spot is to be found anywhere, scarcely a place fit for human habitation. But wherever there is an arm of the sea it has very large cities.[13]

While it appears that Adam never travelled to most of Denmark, and to none of Norway or Sweden, he relies heavily on the views of the King of Denmark, Svein Estridsson. What Adam does, though, is give a relatively early view of the Scandinavian countries. Writing about 1075, Adam describes the lands of the north in a way that gives us a sense of how they were viewed by contemporaries. As a Christian and an outsider, Adam clearly filtered the descriptions through a Christian lens.

---

11 Hawhee and Olson, "Pan-Historiography," 92.

12 Hawhee and Olson, "Pan-Historiography," 94.

13 Adam of Bremen, *History of the Archbishops*, 186–87.

Since Denmark was physically connected and juxtaposed to Christian, feudal Germany, it is not surprising that the Danes were the first to adopt Christianity (ca. 975). But this date is all too convenient. Christianity had been known of long before when Scandinavians had served as Roman mercenaries, and an earlier chieftain Harald Klak had been baptized around 826. It wasn't officially declared a Christian country until Harald Bluetooth declared Christianity his religion for a united Denmark and Norway that defined Denmark as the first Christian Nordic kingdom. Having the support of the Christian Europeans gave Harald valuable allies to consolidate his power. As the Danish National Museum points out "After Harald Bluetooth had been baptized, it was harder for the German Emperors to interfere in Danish affairs."[14] It also further opened the north to Christian writing (i.e. Latin) and classical culture. Moreover, this also led to the spreading of feudal ideas into the north, which historically had been very independent minded and less rigidly hierarchical than their neighbours to the south.

The changes in Denmark were not immediate ones. Latin didn't completely replace literacy in writing. Nordic runestones now appeared with Christian symbols, and funeral stones now embedded "God help his soul" (*Guð hjalpi sál hans*) on the rockface. In fact, the Jelling Stones in Jutland are regarded as some of the finest and best-preserved stones in existence. Denmark still remained fundamentally a pre-Christian Nordic country for the next few hundred years until the complete conversion was achieved. Nor did the conversion stop Viking raids. Monasteries were less frequently targeted, but raids on towns were still conducted for booty and supplies. Yet having a Nordic country converted gave a base for missionaries to attempt further conversion of the north.

Years later, in the early 1200s, Saxo Grammaticus outlined the history of the Danes from their mythological past to the present time of his writing. He describes the history of the people there to establish a national identity. Since he, himself, was a Dane, this is clearly a work of national importance to the kingdom. Saxo synthesizes historical accounts, Latinate tradition of literature, and oral and written stories from various other countries, but particularly Icelandic sources, to recount the makings of the Danish Kingdom.

---

14 National Museet, "The Transition to Christianity."

Sweden

North and East of the Jutland peninsula lies Sweden. One of the earliest references to the Swedes comes from the *Beowulf* manuscript, in which, after Beowulf's death, Wīglaf worries that the cowardice of the Geats who have fled the dragon's wrath will show the Swedes that the Geats are cowards.

> So this bad blood between us and the Swedes,
> this vicious feud, I am convinced,
> is bound to revive; they will cross our borders
> and attack in force when they find out
> that Beowulf is dead. In days gone by
> when our warriors fell and we were undefended
> he kept our coffers and our kingdom safe.[15]

> Þæt ys sīo fæhðo   ond se fēondscipe,
> wæl-nið wera   ðæs ðe ic wēn hafo,
> þē ūs sēceað tō   Swēona lēoda,
> syððan hīe gefricgeað   frēan ūserne
> ealdor-lēasne,   þone ðe ær gehēold
> wið hettendum   hord ond rīce
> æfter hæleða hryre,[16]

The poem ends with an elegiac note because the Geats are doomed without their champion to save them. This analysis of the Swedish dominance of the landscape appears to be an accurate assessment from the *Beowulf* poet, since the Swedish people dominated the lands north of Jutland in the medieval period.

Additionally, Ibn Fadlan travelled north into what is now modern-day Russia. In the Kingdom of the Khazars, he met a group of Scandinavians. Since the description and the geographical location are evident, then it is likely these are Swedes Fadlan encountered. His description of them being "like palm trees. They are fair and ruddy...Each of them carries an axe, a sword, and a knife,"[17] and "all their women wear on their bosoms a circular brooch."[18] Fadlan's descriptions match the personal effects of medieval Scandinavians.

It is not surprising that the militarily strong and economically prosperous northern Swedes would catch the interest of early missionaries in the

---

15 *Beowulf*, trans. Heaney, 201, 203.

16 *Beowulf*, trans. Heaney, 200, 202.

17 Ibn Fadlan, *Ibn Fadlan*, 45.

18 Ibn Fadlan, *Ibn Fadlan*, 46.

north. Ansgar, a cleric from the diocese of Hamburg-Bremen, attempted to start a Christian community on the trading site of Birka in Sweden several miles from present-day Stockholm. Ansgar met with some interest, and he did manage to convert a few Swedes, but his mission in 829–831 was ultimately unsuccessful. Ansgar's replacement, Gautbert, seems to have been inept because he was "driven out by a pagan mob."[19] Ansgar returned in 850 to try again, but he was no more successful on his second visit. Despite his preaching and occasional conversions, Sweden remained largely pagan for almost another two hundred years.

Since Sweden was the last to convert to Christianity (ca. 1035), it seems rather odd how positively Adam of Bremen describes Sweden:

> The Swedish country is extremely fertile; the land is rich in fruits and honey besides excelling all others in cattle raising, exceedingly happy instreams and woods, the whole region everywhere full of merchandise from foreign parts...Although all Hyperboreans are noted for their hospitality, our Swedes are so in particular. To deny wayfarers entertainment is to them the basest of all shameful deeds...There are many Swedish peoples, excelling in strength and arms, besides being the best of fighters on horse as well as on ships. This also accounts for their holding the other peoples of the North in their power...nevertheless, the power of these kings depends on the will of the people.[20]

While the Danes sought influence and power by turning south, the Swedes turned east and the riches of the Slavs living along the Volga River. The Swedes traded extensively with the Slavs finally working their way as far as the Crimea on the Black Sea. This pipeline of wealth in Arabic metals and eastern furs made the Swedes a powerful player in the north. I must also clarify that the Swedes were a tribal cultural group that gained supremacy in eastern Scandinavia and the idea of a Sweden as we know it wasn't a reality until the eleventh to twelfth centuries when the Swedes consolidated power in their area. Over the next few hundred years (and some say this friendly rivalry exists even today) the Swedes and Danes vied for supremacy and influence in the north.

---

19 Page, *Chronicles of the Vikings*, 228.

20 Adam of Bremen, *History of the Archbishops*, 203–4.

Norway

Norway is perhaps the most difficult geographical region to control in Scandinavia. It is connected to Sweden, a short boat ride from Denmark and other northern continental countries, yet it is much more geographically difficult because of its great forests and tall mountains. Adam of Bremen describes Norway as something of a backwater.

> As Nortmannia is the farthest country of the world, so we properly place consideration of it the last part of this book. By moderns it is called Norway. Of its location and extent, we made some mention earlier in connection with Sweden. But this in particular must now be said, that in its length that land extends into the farthest northern zone, whence also it takes its name. It begins with towering crags at the sea commonly called the Baltic; then with its main ridge bent north, after following the course of the shore line of a raging ocean, it finally has its bounds in the Riphean Mountains, where the tired world also comes to an end. On account of the roughness of its mountains and the immoderate cold, Norway is the most unproductive of all countries...Poverty has forced them thus to go all over the world and from piratical raids they bring home in great abundance the riches of the lands.[21]

What is important to note is that Adam of Bremen is pointing out that the Norwegians went trading and on raids as a by-product of their geography. For them, it was a matter of survival because of the short growing season, isolated geography, and relative lack of agricultural production.

To accommodate this trading and raiding, the Norwegian shipbuilding became a strong industry. Of all of the Scandinavian countries, Norway had the great forests to provide raw lumber for shipbuilding. This material culture became important for transporting both traders and war parties across Europe. The Scandinavian ship builders are considered some of the very best. While the other Europeans were leery of venturing too far out to sea in their ships, the Viking Knörr and longships routinely crossed the North Sea, Baltic, and North Atlantic. Their shiplap and inner framework proved to be a good design for traversing heavy seas.

Surprisingly, even though the settlements of Norway were isolated and difficult to travel between, Christian missionaries braved the hostile climate and geography to work on conversion, yet the historical data concerning the conversion are somewhat nebulous. Adam of Bremen and Saxo Grammaticus both chronicled Christian missionary work in the north. Robert Ferguson contends that the seep of Christianity took a long time, starting with Håkon the Good's son Harald Fairhair (Harald *hárfagri*) who was fostered to

---

21 Adam of Bremen, *History of the Archbishops*, 210–11.

a Christian king, Athelstan, in England. However, Harald's efforts to convert Norway were mostly ineffectual.[22] Even though the initial incursion of Christianity took place around 975, the country remained mostly pagan. Even with the efforts of King Olaf Tryggvason (ca. 995), Norway was only nominally Christian. Even though Tryggvason had Leif Erickson baptized, and that helped spread Christianity in Iceland and Greenland, Olaf didn't endear himself to his people. He destroyed pagan temples and forced conversion when he could. After several years of this, his country remained unsympathetic to Christian teachings. King Olaf II Haraldsson (1015–1028), known as St. Olaf, was even more harsh in his conversion practices. His attempts at conversion were ruthless and earned him the name "Olaf the Lawbreaker" since he didn't follow established laws and customs in Norway. While he was overzealous in the conversion of Norway, his population was considerably less so. In fact, it was not until 1154 that the pope considered Norway sufficiently Christian to deserve an archdiocese.

This timeline also shows that classical culture would not have been widely spread throughout Norway until long after Harald Fairhair's attempts at Christianity—even long after Saint Olaf's reign (1015–1028). Traditional pagan practices were still commonly used until the Christian, classical models finally displaced them, which was a longer process encompassing several generations.

The Expansion Period, The Settlement of Iceland, and The Diaspora

As with other sea-faring peoples, the medieval Scandinavians settled many lands and started many colonies. During this expansion period, the Scandinavians found themselves in a bind. Their population growth had risen to strain their resources, so moving on to settle more abundant areas was almost inevitable. Much like the Greeks and Phoenicians, the medieval Scandinavians found themselves needing to expand so that their population burden wouldn't break their society. Additionally, some colonists fled the encroachment of both the feudal structure, which threatened their traditional forms of self-rule, and Christianity, which also attempted to break their traditional religion. Their technology of shipbuilding gave the people the ability to travel great distances to establish both trading posts and new settlements.

---

22 Ferguson, *The Vikings*, 263–64.

The Orkney Islands were a place of strategic importance to the British Isles. Before the attacks on Lindisfarne in 793, the island was settled by Irish monks and Gaelic peoples. When the Scandinavians began their raids on the poorly defended monasteries in England, the Orkneys became a strategic point with which to launch their raids. Archaeological evidence is scarce as to whether the Norse settling in the Orkneys came there as conquerors or whether they came as peaceful farmers and traders. One point is clear—the Norse completely displaced the native population and renamed the older Gaelic place names with Scandinavian ones.

The *Orkneyinga Saga* follows up this early history with the founding of Orkney as a jarldom. According to the saga, Harald Fairhair gave the Orkneys to Jarl Rognvald for the loss of his son in service to the king. But since Rognvald already held lands in Norway, and didn't want to give them up, Rognvald gave these lands to his brother, Sigurd, who became the first jarl of Orkney.

The importance of the diaspora here is that this settlement in the Orkneys occurred early in the Viking Age, and the Nordic influence went on to affect not only the Orkney Isles, but the Shetlands, parts of Scotland, and many of the islands off the Scottish coast. This culture affected the geographical area for the next several hundred years.

The settlement period of Iceland is well documented by the Icelandic historian Ari Thorgilsson in the *Íslendingabók* (ca. 1125) and the *Landnámabók* (date uncertain, but probably around the early twelfth century). Ari writes in the *Landnámabók* that the settlement period lasted from about 870 to 930. At that time, most of the land had been claimed, and farmsteads arose around the edges of Iceland since glaciers or artic deserts occupied the middle of the island. Ingólfr Arnarson is said to have founded the Icelandic capital of Reykjavík in 874. Tradition holds that Arnarson threw two logs, which would later serve to build his high seat, off of his ship as he reached the shores of Iceland. A year later, his slaves found the poles washed up in a smoky bay[23] in southwest Iceland. He established a farm here, and it later became the village where Reykjavík is now located. His story is one of the most important to Icelanders because he represents the founding of the country—and still has an impact on modern Icelanders.

Iceland became an interesting example of medieval Scandinavian lifestyle. Fleeing from the encroaching feudal and Christian institutions, Iceland kept many of the old cultural structures which were eventually written down in their sagas. As Hawhee and Olson describe in their essay, "Pan-Historiography," connecting the dots of a large swath of time and geographical space

---

23 Reykjavík literally means smoky bay. Reykja= smoke and vík= bay.

can be enriched and enlivened by slicing down to particular places, people, or events.[24] Examining Iceland and its sagas provides the slicing in to look at a particular culture that best represents a later look at what earlier Scandinavian culture looked like. Icelandic culture and language are conservative, and people with a good knowledge of Icelandic can read Old Norse. Many of the best-preserved sagas are from Iceland. Bringing the slicing metaphor of Hawhee and Olson to bear on the Icelandic sagas helps us better understand the legal and civic rhetorics in the medieval Nordic world. The rhetorical dominance of *hóf*, a rhetoric of reasonableness, permeated both civic and legal rhetoric of the day.

The isolated nature of Iceland makes it a perfect exemplar for looking at the medieval Nordic culture. The rhetorical stances of peace and violence in the native population are of particular importance since so much of the perceptions of the Vikings were the violence directed outward to other places they attacked. According to Straumsheim's research, medieval Iceland was one of the more peaceful places in Europe. He identifies the cultural constructs that limit the use of violence. He directly points to Iceland's mediation system and legal system when looking at the ways political violence was avoided. "Such an approach to conflict resolution in most cases resolved disputes quickly and to the satisfaction of the parties."[25] The idea of *hóf*, or reasonableness, was predicated on keeping a civil and legal peace in a place lacking a central bureaucratic government. For instance, when Christianity was introduced in Iceland, the new religion wasn't openly accepted, and only after several years of proselytizing did the issue of Christian and pagan reach a level where violence might occur. Instead of a religious war, the two parties went to court and plead their cases. The law-speaker at the *Alþing* circa the year 1000 was "Thorgeir of Ljosavatn, who held office for seventeen years and though a heathen announced the adoption of Christianity in Iceland."[26] Thorgeir did, however, declare that pagans could still practice their religion in private and that Christian eating habits (e.g., the banning of eating horse flesh) would not influence Iceland. This way, both parties in the case received something. On a practical level, it took the pressure off of Iceland to convert, and it stopped Norway or Denmark from invading in order to convert the Icelanders.

---

24 Hawhee and Olson, "Pan-Historiography," 91–94.

25 Straumsheim, "Peacemaking in the Middle Ages."

26 Jones, *History of the Vikings*, 283.

The sagas also tell of the founding of the colony in Greenland. The *Grœn-lendinga Saga* and *Eirík's Saga Rauða* (*Erik the Red's Saga*) relate the story of settling Greenland in isolated colonies, their adventures and expeditions further west, and the discovery of Vinland, North America, in L'Anse Aux Meadows, Nova Scotia. These sagas tell us about the environment and the conditions of exploration and life in the westernmost parts of the north Atlantic. We also learn of the spread of Christianity there from Leif Eirikson, who brought Christianity with him from Norway to Greenland—although there were probably Christians there, and people who knew of the religion before he edified it.

At the same time settlers were fleeing from Norway to Iceland, ca. 870 to 930, the Faroe Islands were also settled. Much like the Orkneys, the Norse settlers displaced Irish monks who had travelled there to live solitary, ascetic lives. The archaeological evidence suggests that a rather large number of settlers arrived in a rather short period of time. This meant that the islands must have been known beforehand, but the relative isolation made them a desirable target for emigrants fleeing Harald Fairhair, since the Faroes are much closer than Iceland. The evidence suggests that Norse farming methods and lifestyle were maintained on the Faroes. Longhouses and several *þing* sites have been discovered, and there is a close linguistic relationship between Faroese and both Old Norse and modern Icelandic.

The story of the Faroes's conversion to Christianity in 999 is more tragic and violent than that of Iceland, yet it may have led the impetus for Iceland's peaceful adoption of Christianity. The *Faereyinga Saga* tells the tale of Olaf Tryggvason, sending one of his jarls, Sigmundr Brestisson to bring Christianity to the Faroes. Instead of introducing the positives of the new faith, Sigmundr tried to force the population to convert by the sword. His destruction of pagan temples and imposition of the new religion on the populace was met with vigorous resistance. The rebel leader, Þrándr í Götu, led an ill-fated revolt which was defeated, and Christianity became the religion of the Faroes.

Conclusion

As this research has shown, the history and context of the Viking Age shows a people who were defined in many ways by their geographical position on the edge of the classically influenced Christian Europe. The Scandinavians had their own laws, culture, and civic practices that were slowly subsumed by Christian Europe as the medieval period gave way to the later Middle Ages. Moreover, it is still possible to deduce some of the civic and legal rhetoric by using the Icelandic sagas and Nordic law codes as exempla of the older systems. The story captured by the saga writers, of the native traditions in the medieval north, is one of loss and remembrance. In these sagas, we see *hóf* as a cultural stance in their rhetoric to keep the peace and create functioning systems of small, isolated civic bureaucracies. In later years, major nation states emerged to control vast areas of land and sea and the independent people living in small Norse villages saw their way of life change forever.

Chapter 4

THE RHETORIC OF PRAISING AND SHAMING IN THE VIKING WORLD

A wise man does all things in moderation
Gisli Sursson's Saga[1]

FROM AN OUTSIDER'S point of view, especially that of the Christian chroniclers of the day, the medieval Nordic people seemed ignorant and violent. After all, many of the church chroniclers had heard about the Nordic attacks on monasteries along the North Sea coasts. However, in looking at the sagas, as well as the historical and archaeological evidence, this view becomes particularly problematic. Most medieval Scandinavians led relatively peaceful lives as farmers. Since the Scandinavian towns and villages were rather sparsely populated and remote, the need for collective action to survive long harsh winters was of the utmost importance. Thus, rather than construct a society built on violence, the society needed to be peaceful and cooperative so that the group could survive. Saga manuscripts chronicling the early settlement of Iceland show this in effect. Feud is always a possibility, but the sagas show there were many methods to hand by which society could try to diffuse potentially violent situations.

When historians focus on feud, what they are missing is the rhetorical stances of the people *before* any violence ensues, and the actions of other citizens to help end the violence if it starts. The main rhetorical stance of the medieval Nordic peoples was the idea of *hóf*,[2] the idea of reasonableness as a means of keeping the peace and ensuring their collective survival as a group. Rhetoric for the Norse was a means by which a reasonable solution could, and should, be reached between parties in a way that saved face for

---

[1] *Gisli Sursson's Saga*, trans. Regal and Quinn, 26.

[2] The Old Norse Prose Dictionary Project lists terms related to *hóf* and their number of usages. *Hóf*, for instance, is used 136 times in the sagas. References to *ójafnaðarmaðr* and unevenness of character are used 59 times while *drengr*, an honourable and ideal man, is used 155 times. The legal term *lögmaðr* appears 118 times. *Ójafn*, meaning uneven, is used 34 times. *Níðr* is used over 130 times. Of the terms for friendship, *vinfengi*, is used 57 times while *vinátta* appears 85 times. Even the women's term for friendship *vinkona* appears 19 times. For further information, see the *Dictionary of Old Norse Prose*, https://onp.ku.dk/onp/onp.php?

everyone involved. The social structure was set up for this: society placed a high value on people who were reasonable, and shamed those who were seen as being unreasonable, or, *óhóf*.[3] To understand this in a larger context, it is necessary to understand the difference and implications of a shame culture versus a guilt one, and why this is important for understanding the civic rhetoric of the medieval Scandinavians.

Hóf appears as a set of principles to which the individual should aspire. Reasonableness is praised in many sagas as a way to conduct oneself in public dealings, since *hóf* brought stability to smaller decentralized areas in Scandinavia. Kristen Wolf argues that this value was important across all demographics in all Scandinavia. "The need for moderation in eating, drinking, and even wisdom, and the value of circumspection in one's dealings with others are emphasized."[4] Saga literature often shows threats to Icelandic peace and stability by men who demonstrate *óhóf*, or unreasonableness.

> The sagas have a specific term for ruthless and overly ambitious men. They are called *ójafnaðarmenn* (sing. *ójafnaðarmaðr*) meaning "uneven," unjust, or overbearing men. *Ójafnaðarmenn* took advantage of the fact that social defenses against a thoroughly ruthless individual were cumbersome and potentially inadequate.[5]

These men are often the villainous people described in the sagas. If the rhetoric of reasonableness was valued in the society, it makes sense that the sagas would cast this negative trait in a negative light to show the future readers the conduct that is valued in the society. The sagas reinforce positive social interactions by showing and commenting on the negative societal impacts of the *ójafnaðarmenn*.

Men who are civic minded and respectful in keeping the peace are often referred to in the sagas as *jafn*, or even-minded men. They are thoughtful and willing to reasonably act in public matters openly and with good intent. In contrast to them are the *ójafnaðarmaðr*—men of uneven temper. The idea of a reciprocal balance sheet sometimes influenced the Old Norse saga landscape. When the uneven man has pushed too far, or offended too much, the civic responsibility of a reasonable man is to balance those scales, to get even.

An impactful example of this comes from the *Ljósvetninga Saga*. The saga opens with a description of people who are viewed positively—Thorgeir the

---

3 In Old Norse, the prefix Ó- represents a negation, so the term *óhóf* literally means "not reasonable."

4 Wolf, *Viking Age*, 70.

5 Byock, *Feud in the Icelandic Saga*, 29–30.

Chieftain, Forni, Arnor, Thorfinn. The description of these men is a coun-terexample to the descriptions of the antagonists in the saga—the brothers Solmund, Soxolf, and Eyjolf. While Andersson and Miller view the contrast as a "juxtaposition of good and evil,"[6] the better contrast, to my mind, is between *hóf* and *óhóf*. Later, Andersson and Miller comment that the con-trast emerges between moderate and immoderate conduct. The brothers are described in the saga as "all forceful and overbearing men" who were "great troublemakers."[7] The language of the saga consistently draws the comparison of reasonableness versus unreasonableness in the character-ization of the major figures of the saga, and the intention is clearly to show how civil society is damaged by the actions of the immoderate men. Their cultural mores determined a lot of their social and legal actions.

Guilt Culture Versus Shame Culture

In the hypermasculine world of the sagas, honour is a major motivation in all civic dealings. To save face and keep one's honour intact are extremely important motivating factors in the dealings with fellow villagers or coun-trymen. Transgressions against this public "face" could bring dishonour or shame—something anyone in that society would be loath to endure. Guerra and colleagues point out the multifunction of a shame-based culture in rela-tion to a code of honour in regulating civic activity.

> Pitt-Rivers (2001) suggests the existence of three basic functions of an honor code: (1) it guides one's judgment and moral evaluations of others; (2) it influences one's own actions before society; and (3) it is a measure of social status. Consequently, honor is one's own image and, at the same time, the representation of one's moral values in the social group. In this sense, it is an integrated part of a group's social identity (Pitt-Rivers, 2003), being present in the interpersonal relationships established in the group.[8]

The shame culture is often associated in cultural anthropology with honour cultures. The Germanic peoples—the medieval Nordic peoples included—practiced shame culture. This meant that ethics and morality were publicly constructed and driven. For instance, a person contemplating an action might view the dynamics in terms of what society would think of him if he committed the action. But fundamental to this type of culture is public perception of an individual's behaviour. The public view of the person was

---

6 Andersson and Miller, *Law and Literature*, 99.

7 Andersson and Miller, *Law and Literature*, 122.

8 Guerra, et al., "The Importance of Honor," 299.

important. To be accepted and have good standing in the community, the person's public honour needed to be maintained at all costs, and this led to appropriate behaviour to avoid being shamed or ostracized from the community. In many older cultures, this might be the equivalence of a death sentence, since without a clan, tribe, or community, the individual has no safety net. Shweder notes that

> Socially shared and valued ego ideals, notions about a well-developed self, and ideas about what it means to be a good, worthy, admirable, attractive, or competent person are variable across time and space; and as they vary, the character, substance and meaning of "shame" can be expected to vary as well, although not in an unlimited number of ways.[9]

Thus, the idea of a shame culture is socially constructed to fit that society's notions of what is good and proper publicly.

This emphasis on praise for acts the public deems worthy and shame for acts that public consensus says falls short of collective expectations may seem much like Aristotle's definition of the epideictic. When Aristotle wrote about the types of rhetoric, he explains that the epideictic centres on praise and blame, and that it concerns the present (as opposed to the future or past), but as Cynthia Sheard points out, "epideictic discourse was burdened from the start by suspicions of the speaker's self-indulgence and opportunism, his manipulation of audience sentiments, and his distance from the interests of the community."[10] The medieval Scandinavians didn't use praise and blame in Aristotle's meaning of the word. They used the variation of praise and shame. While this praise and shame culture seems like a form of epideictic, several points of difference must be made. Praise and shame cultures share many similarities to the epideictic, but the suspicious view of epideictic as lacking importance does not apply to the Nordic praise and shame culture.

Due to the praise and shame structures of the society shown in the sagas, *topoi* seem to exist for both praise and shaming situations. Goading, for instance, creates *topoi* for shame situations for different contexts and power relations. Public praising or shaming is a conscious rhetorical move to spur someone to action. Praising and shaming moved medieval Scandinavians to action, thus, showing that praise and shame cultures use this as an active form of rhetoric to instigate civic action.

Sociological approaches have looked at shame cultures in terms of societal norms and the pressure on the individual to meet those norms. In shame cultures, people judge their actions through an external lens where the indi-

---

9 Shweder, "Toward a Deep Cultural Psychology," 1120.
10 Sheard, "The Public Value of Epideictic Rhetoric," 767–68.

vidual needs to be aware of public audience for actions and the social consequences for doing/not doing something. In these cultures, the moral compass of the society is external to the person. Societal values viewed socially determine what is right and wrong. In this case, the transgressor is judged by others, not the self. If something bad happened, and the community didn't know, then there would be no shame until the transgression was brought to light. From a modern perspective, it is very constraining to worry about the needs of the external when it may interfere with individual motivation. In some instances, it raises "the other" above "the self" when matters of public action are considered. According to Heller,

> The bearer of the social triggers of shame is the eye of the Other, the eye of the community. One is constantly seen whatever one is doing; one is supposed to be seen. If she carries out all activities according to the norms or rules of the community, she is not ashamed for the Eye approves. However, if she is doing something that infringes the rules, or at least might be seen as something that infringes them, the affect of shame conquers or possesses the person. Whenever the eye of the Other disapproves, the guilty party feels annihilated: she blushes, bends her head so she cannot see the judgment of the Eye, runs away or at least feels the urge to disappear or sink into the earth in order not be seen.[11]

In any heroic society, the idea of words and deeds carries with it the potential for praise or shame. In Viking culture public words were considered carefully since they might bring the speaker shame if an utterance was in haste, ill-thought out, or damaging to another person's reputation. Honour, public honour, meant everything. A man, or family, or clan were only as honourable as their words. The code of conduct constructed for the functioning society had to be obeyed. Failing to live up to an obligation in a public arena brought shame. In Icelandic sources, the shame culture is preserved in its original intent of civic regulation of activities. This element is clear in the sagas post-conversion, which lends relevance to the ideas of Byock and others that the sagas preserve native, historic traditions.

It is now beneficial to turn towards the idea of a guilt culture as a means of contrast. Guilt culture in European history is generally viewed as a Christian phenomenon. It is a change of focus in matters of morality. Christianity laid out many prescriptive laws, judgements, and strictures which the congregations needed to follow. Whether each individual followed these rules was not always a matter of public knowledge. The lists of "thou shalt nots" in Christianity is extensive. Nevertheless, the guilt culture creates the stan-

---

11 Heller, "Five Approaches," 1019.

dard the individual must follow. Rather than an outside lens to view codes of conduct as worthy or unworthy, the guilt culture creates an internal lens with which to view your own adherence to the laws and codes of conduct the individual finds worthy. Failure to live up to this code creates internal anguish (guilt), so punishment in the guilt culture is from within. People suffer because they expect to be punished. In the early Christian sense, punishment through damnation or suffering was expected of those who breached moral teachings. It does not need societal judgement on the merits of action or inaction. The internalized guilt does the judging of the action.

Critics in the twentieth century viewed the switch from a shame to a guilt culture as a natural evolution in morality. To them, the guilt culture of Christianity swiftly replaced shame as a means of societal control. Once again, we see the clash of a Christian and pagan worldview where the Christian narrative of superiority is held up against an earlier civic structure. David Konstan's essay, "Shame in Ancient Greece," acknowledges the problem in looking at older Greek texts—which is relevant to the study of post-conversion medieval peoples as well.

> Shame has had a bad press for the past century or so. As Thomas Scheff remarks...'Over the last 200 years in the history of modern societies, shame virtually disappeared. The denial of shame has been institutionalized in Western societies.' Shame's status as a moral emotion has been impugned by critics, among them theologians and anthropologists, who consider it a primitive precursor to guilt: shame, the argument goes, responds to the judgments of others and is indifferent to ethical principles in themselves, whereas guilt is an inner sensibility and corresponds to the morally autonomous self of modern man. The shift from a shame culture to a guilt culture, in the formula made popular by Ruth Benedict (1946), is taken as a sign of moral progress. Thus the warrior society represented in the Homeric epics—a shame culture, according to E. R. Dodds (1951)—slowly gave way to a guilt culture, which began to emerge in fifth-century democratic Athens but did not achieve a fully developed expression in the classical world until the advent of Christianity.[12]

The narrative that societal structures were lacking until Christianity came to rescue the world is troubling and problematic. It assumes that the civic structures set in place were so ill-equipped to serve a functioning society that the guilt culture of Christianity quickly fixed the problems of the primitive pre-Christian civilization. This was not true of any of the structures Christianity replaced. They were different, but not savage, primitive, or other pejoratives applied to them. And since these other structures were not lacking, the

---

12 Konstan, "Shame in Ancient Greece," 1031.

idea they were quickly replaced by guilt culture is also fallacious. The Greek and Roman shame cultures weren't replaced in a day, and neither were the Germanic ones. Bjork and Niles argue the point in respect to the Beowulf manuscript being created for a Christian audience by a Christian poet, and therefore, enforcing Christian themes. George Clark points out that,

> The introduction of a new state-sanctioned (or ruler-sanctioned) religion does not necessarily effect radical change in a culture's basic structure of values. Not only in *Beowulf* but the *Maxims* of the Exeter Book—"Dom bið selast" (Fame is best)—and the *Battle of Maldon* attest to the vitality of the shame culture and its values in Anglo-Saxon England long after the Conversion.[13]

The sagas attest to this fact as well. Even though the sagas were written down after the conversion of Iceland, they still retain and embody the cultural values of the shame culture and the rhetorical principles involved with it.[14]

The sagas and elements of skaldic poetry exhibit many cases of praise and shame cultural artifacts. Starting with praise as a cultural ideal, the uses of praise poetry, the *drápa*, and instances it afforded in the saga manuscripts, suggests a clear line between what was considered acceptable to society and what was deemed bad behaviour. Praise and shame, then, become a vehicle for public, civic rhetoric. While these ideas of praise and shame may contrast with some modern beliefs, to the mind of the medieval Scandinavian, these ideas were a web that helped bring honour and, for the most part, kept peace in the small village structure found throughout the medieval Nordic world.

Examining Civic Rhetoric in the North

In the medieval north during the Viking Age, before the creep of feudal Europe and Christianity, the civic culture was based on a praise and shame culture. The societies did not have a strong central government, and they needed other ways to maintain an active public culture. The small settle-

---

13 Clark, "The Hero and the Theme," 285.

14 Reinsma's essay "Rhetoric in England: The Age of Ælfric, 970–1020," exposes the lack of Continental rhetorical concepts during the Benedictine Revival. By exploring the Old English corpus of Christian rhetorical documents in England, he argues that there isn't a strong manuscript tradition for Christian, Classical rhetoric at the time. Most of Ælfric's work seems to have come from encyclopedic compendia and not from original source material. Reinsma concludes that, perhaps, churchmen in England at the time didn't realize the potential of Christian and Classical models of rhetoric. If this is the case, then the implications for the Scandinavians who were converted much later seem to suggest a lack of Continental rhetorical knowledge.

ments and lack of resources needed a cooperative populace to ensure survival for everyone. To do this, they created civic structures based on cooperative principles that transcended class and gender. The ideals of these principles were public, and the people were responsible for holding each other to the agreed standards. The webs of civic rhetoric touched everything from court cases to interactions between remote farmers.

People who upheld these values were praised. They embodied the values of the society. Skalds, the northern poets, created poems to exemplify these cultural icons. Men who were moderate, loyal, oath-keepers, and respected the law were considered *drengskapr*. Those who were selfish, uneven, and immoderate were often labelled *ójafn* or *níðingr*. Their reputations and their family's reputation were tarnished in the public eye.

This form of civic-cultural policing required everyone on the farm, the *goðorð* where the *goði* held sway, and the villages to take an active part in civic matters. If the people let a person get away with immoderate behaviour they risked having the repercussions spread across the countryside and perhaps endanger their own safety or survival. The public nature of the civic discourse of the medieval Scandinavian people was successful because it brought people together and formed bonds of cooperation. The language used had to be public, and it had to stress reciprocity in the relationship. The society worked well as long as everyone owed each other some form of civic duty. When someone broke these bonds of public accountability, public shaming was the way to bring these immoderate people back into the fold.

Praise

In the world of the heroic epic, there was nothing greater than the public honour of praise. Throughout the ancient world, from Ancient Greece through the Middle Ages, praise from your community was considered best. The medieval Norse were no exception. The right action or gesture could bring public accolades which would enhance one's honour and prestige. The outward filter on praise means that people weren't necessarily judged on their moral fibre of character, but on how well they navigated the idea of public perception. The average person could probably function well in a society like this, while a few savvy individuals would find it advantageous to build their prestige through publicly seen "good deeds." Only those who couldn't resist the temptation to commit acts that they knew were probably wrong would deviate from the norms of society and commit shameful acts.

Drengr, Drengskapr, and Drápa as Rhetoric

The sagas portray a clear heroic stance on praise. The Old Norse term *drengr* can be defined as a warrior and as a cultural ideal. Snorri Sturluson's *Skáldskaparmál* describes this as, "Manly and ambitious men are called drengir."[15] It is often used as a term of praise in the sagas. The Vikings viewed the warrior ideal as praiseworthy and manly, and they often used martial terms when granting praise. These terms of praise often refer to bravery, fairness, a sense of duty to honourable acts, and forbearance in battle. In *The Story of the Heath Slayings*, Thorbiorn has his foot chopped off in a fight with Bardi. When Thorbiorn fails to concede the fight Bardi calls him a troll, but Thorbiorn answers, "nought of trollship is it for a man to bear his wounds, and not to be so soft as to forbear warding him while he may. That may be accounted for manliness rather."[16] Thorbiorn's efforts as a *drengr* impressed the other warriors and the scene ends with "There he fell and earned a good word."[17]

In *The Saga of Gunnlaug Serpent-Tongue*, When Gunnlaug travels to Norway, Earl Eirik Hakonarson notices a problem with Gunnlaug's foot.

> "What's the matter with your foot, Icelander?" the earl asked.
> "I have a boil on it, my lord," he replied.
> "But you weren't limping?"
> "One mustn't limp while both legs are the same length," Gunnlaug replied.[18]
>
> Jarl mælti: "Hvat er fæti þínum, íslendingr?"
> "Sullr er á, herra," sagði hann.
> "Ok gekk þú þó ekki haltr?"
> Gunnlaugr svarar: "Eigi skal haltr ganga, meðan báðir fætr eru jafnlangir."[19]

Gunnlaug's forbearance of pain shows his manly nature which should have drawn praise from his hosts; yet one of the earl's followers doesn't recognize this and sets things in motion to cause problems for Gunnlaug later in the saga.

Perhaps the greatest warrior poet of the sagas, Egil Skallagrimsson is the ultimate ideal. He is a warrior of great skill and a poet of great renown, and he ventures through his saga praising his friends and shaming his enemies. Even the Old Norse term *drengskapr*, taken from the root for war-

---

15 Sturluson, *The Prose Edda*, trans. Faulkes, 151.

16 *The Story of the Heath Slayings*, trans. Morris and Magnusson, 46.

17 *The Story of the Heath Slayings*, trans Morris and Magnusson, 46.

18 "The Saga of Gunnlaug Serpent-Tongue," trans. Attwood, 571.

19 *Gunnlaugs saga ormstungu*, The Icelandic Saga Database.

rior, refers to nobleness, honour, and high-mindedness. To be brave, noble, and puissant is to be a *drengskapr*. The Icelandic skalds, their poets, were responsible for upholding this ideal. If a warrior upheld the *drengskapr*, they would often compose *drápa*, or long verse poems dedicated to the deeds of the great warriors. The skald is a major force in developing praise through verse. There are several instances in Norse poetry of *drápa*: The *Knútsdrápa* telling the exploits of Cnut the great and the mythological *Þórsdrápa* poem of deeds of the god Thor. In *Egil's Saga*, Egil often used the *drápa* to praise people with whom he wanted to reconcile.

From the time Egil was a child of three, he had the gift of poetry. When he was just a boy, Egil wasn't allowed to go with his father, Skallagrim, and the other householders to Yngvar's hall for a feast since his father said there would be excessive drinking. So Egil stole a horse and rode to the feast anyway against his father's wishes. Yngvar greeted the little boy and Egil composed this short *drápa*,

I have come in fine fettle to the hearth	Kominn emk enn til arna
of Yngvar, who gives men gold from the glowing	Yngvars, þess's beð lyngva,
curled serpent's bed of heather;	hann vask fúss at finna,
I was eager to meet him.	fránþvengjar gefr drengjum.
Shedder of gold rings bright and twisted	Mun eigi þú, þægir,
from the serpent's realm, you'll never	þrévetran mér betra,
find a better craftsman of poems	ljósundinna landa
three winters old than me.[20]	linns, óðar smið finna.[21]

This use of praise is quite savvy for the child. He praises the host as being generous and a *goði* who gives gold gifts to his retainers. This poem at a feast publicly praising the host would give Yngvar honour, and it would also create honour for Egil as the poet, but also for his father, Skallagrim. The father must have been furious at Egil for disregarding his order to stay home, but the public honour he received probably helped Egil avoid too much punishment.

Egil often found poetry making a way to mitigate hostility and conflict he continually found himself in. When he and his friend Arinbjorn stood before King Eirik Bloodaxe to make peace for killing retainers of Eirik, Egil composed a *drápa* praising the king's prowess in battle.

---

20 *Egil's Saga*, trans. Scudder, 52.
21 *Egils saga*, The Icelandic Saga Database.

The clash of swords roared	Óx hjörva glöm
on the edge of shields,	við hlífar þröm.
battle grew around the king,	Guðr óx of gram.
fierce he ventured forth.	Gramr sótti fram.
The bloodriver raced,	Þar heyrðisk þá,
The din was heard then	þaut mækis á,
of metal showered in battle,	malmhríðar spá.
the most in that land	Sú vas mest of lá.
The web of spears	Vasat villr staðar
did not stray from their course	vefr darraðar
above the king's	of grams glaðar
bright row of shields.	geirvangs raðar.
The shore groaned,	Þars í blóði
pounded by the flood	enn brimlá-móði
of blood, resounded	völlr of þrumði,
under the banners' march	und véum glumði.
In the mud men lay	Hné folk á fit
when spears rained down.	við fleina hnit.
Eirik that day	Orðstír of gat
won great renown.[22]	Eiríkr at þat.[23]

This excerpt shows the *drápa* as a kind of encomium for the hero. The aspects of the *drengr* or *drengskapr* are prominently displayed in the poetry. Eirik Bloodaxe showed *drenskapr*. He waded into battle, and he didn't back down. His shield was raised high, and the blood of his opponents washed the ground. Egil's *drápa* praised the king in a public way to show the honour Egil was giving him.

The public nature of praise is important to understand since the rhetorical act of praising here is seen as an act of contrition by praising someone you had been in conflict with. The nature of public praise cannot be overstated. The poet who praises a person with a *drápa*, or the person who publicly praises someone for good deeds is reinforcing a publicly constructed and generally believed to be the best kind of behaviour for someone in that society. If the person getting praised truly earned it, then his reputation, and thus, his honour, would increase among the citizens. It would bring accolades to his family and farmstead. It would also increase the reputation for the one giving the praise—whether that was a skald or a member of the community. Rightly praising someone would be looked upon as a good deed.

---

22 *Egil's Saga*, trans. Scudder, 115.

23 *Egils saga*, The Icelandic Saga Database.

Later in the saga, the older Egil composes this *drápa* to his ally Arinbjorn as a gift for his new position in the royal court. This is just a brief excerpt:

By my side, better	Þar stóð mér
than every other	mörgum betri
spreader of treasure,	hoddfíöndum
stood my loyal friend	á hlið aðra
whom I truly trusted,	tryggr vinr minn,
growing in stature	sás trúa knáttak,
with his every deed.	heiðþróaðr
	hverju ráði,
Arinbjorn,	Arinbjörn,
paragon of men,	es oss einn of hóf,
who lifted me alone	knía fremstr,
above the king's anger.	frá konungs fjónum,
The king's friend,	vinr þjóðans,
who never told untruth	es vættki ló
in the warlike	í herskás
ruler's hall.[24]	hilmis garði.[25]

Once again, we see Egil using his poetry to create praise of character for his friend he intends to praise. The warrior poet Egil uses this rhetorical move several times in the saga to reinforce the proper character of the warrior spirit and of honourable high-mindedness, which is ironic considering Egil's character at times seems a bit erratic, especially in the rivalry with his brother. Since these poems were for public consumption and recited in the long houses for entertainment, they became a public vehicle for teaching and reinforcing proper behaviour of the warriors. After all, who doesn't want a poem composed of their great deeds? Perhaps this use of praise poetry, demonstrating the primacy of the Nordic ethos of honour but also of examining the proper civic conduct of the time, is what makes *Egil's Saga* a favourite in Scandinavia to this day.

Civic Ethos and Cultural Policing

So how were these civic rhetorics supported and enforced in Nordic society? The easy answer would be to examine skaldic poetry where praise and shame could be poured out through verse, but there is more to value-enforcement than just the poetics. For praise, skalds were often employed to compose *drápa* poetry praising lords and *goði*. In addition, skalds would

---

24 *Egil's Saga*, trans. Scudder, 161.
25 *Egils saga*, The Icelandic Saga Database.

often compose the Viking equivalents of panegyric or elegiac poetry to reinforce the idea of *drengr* or *drengskapr* for fallen warriors or the honoured dead, and they could reinforce shame if a person broke civic code. Their rhetorical power would often cement the ideals of the Norse people.

Since this was a praise and shame society, the communities themselves played an important role in maintaining social norms, peace, and community cohesion. This had to be effected through the rhetoric used and not through violence. The society had rules to maintain a social order in places where strong central rule was often lacking. This required consensus and a willingness to listen and maintain relationships and friendships among neighbours. These small farmsteads and villages acted as public venues for displays of friendship and community, and if someone broke the civic norms, then there were rhetorical structures in places to goad, or shame a person into the "right" course of action. Each member of society, from lowly servants to powerful chieftains, had recourse to rhetorical action to affect a course of action in the community. While continental Europe silenced many voices through the feudal system, medieval Scandinavia set up rudimentary democratic systems to help govern and administer small villages. They needed a concerted effort by all members of these farms and villages to survive in the harsh environment they often found themselves in. To do so, the people needed to develop a civic ethos quite different than what evolved in Christian Europe.

By the Viking Age, the profession of skald was already well established. The skaldic verses used during this time to praise and shame were the *drápa*, longer poems of praise, *flokkr*, shorter poems of praise, and *níðvísur*, poems of shame. These forms were of great consequence to the chieftains and society of the day. Skalds were trained to be poets by apprenticing with other, more experienced poets where they learned intricate meters and various poetical devices, many which are outlined in *The Prose Edda*. Once trained, the poets could travel throughout Scandinavia reciting poems, genealogies, and recorded histories of battles in verse, or composing songs about local happenings. This broad range of travel and knowledge helped secure their social roles, and they often entered into some form of patronage relationship with a strong chieftain or king.

Even though scholars often consider Norway as the birthplace of skalds, in the Viking Age Icelandic skalds became known for their skills. Icelandic poets were highly sought after, and many left for Norway, Sweden, and Denmark at the behest of powerful lords. The demand for skalds across Scandinavia showed how much power they had in cultural knowledge and thus policing of that culture. Skalds could produce poems of praise or shame for acts conducted. They commanded a high degree of social power. A well performed *drápa* or *níðvísur* could radically affect someone. Even a king or powerful chieftain could feel the power of these poets. Often the skalds created poems of praise to their patrons in court, but there must have been times where the opposite happened since the Icelandic law code, the *Grágás*, banned *níðvísur*, sentencing the offending skalds to outlawry and exile. Yet clearly, to make this law, there must have been cases of humiliation of powerful lords by the skaldic power of poetry. The transgressions the rhetorical *níðvísur* exposed must have been often enough to gain consensus by worried chieftains to declare it illegal.

If even the chieftains feared the power of the verse, then it would have worried a commoner even more. The civic fear of being shamed publicly by a skald would have acted as a type of social deterrent from acting unreasonably. The civic ethos of medieval Scandinavia meant knowing how to navigate the terrain of praise and shame. If a person could avoid any words or deeds which might bring shame to their family, then they were viewed as a productive member of the civic unit: the farmstead, village, or district. But if they couldn't, then they might incur shame.

To construct an ethos of praise and goodwill in the community, the person needed to think hard about the relationships, friendships, and obligations they took on. Ethos meant that the person had to live a reasonable life and demonstrate *hóf* in their personal and public lives. Excess was looked down upon. Too much drinking, greed, and violence was often frowned upon as unreasonable behaviour for a member of the community, and moderate people in the sagas are often given praise because they viewed the group peace and tranquillity above their immediate concerns.

Conclusion

The praise and shame structures in medieval Norse society are important to understanding *hóf* as a rhetorical strategy. The sagas consistently praise people who practice *hóf*, and shame those who are immoderate and unreasonable. Distinguishing the Nordic difference of praise and shame from a more traditional definition of epideictic opens up the analysis and interpretations of rhetorical principles in the medieval north. It is also important to distinguish the shame culture in the north with the more guilt-based culture establishing itself in Christian Europe. These competing moral structures offered different ideals of public and private social behaviour. In Scandinavia, the public shame-based structure helped society function without strong central governments.

Praise was extremely important to the medieval Scandinavians, and it regulated behaviour in the village. To be lauded in the public eye was an honour. Praiseworthy actions were defined by the collective village, rather than the individual. If a man was considered by the village to be very honourable and believed to perform great deeds, then he might be labelled as a *drengr*, a cultural ideal. Once again, the saga corpus displays and comments on figures who have performed great deeds and are considered *drengr*. Nothing could be a greater honour than having a praise poem, a *drápa*, sung about your deeds.

Medieval Nordic poets, the skalds, were able to perform a type of cultural policing. By holding up examples of reasonable, praiseworthy people, and condemning unreasonable ones through their oral poetry. Since the rhetoric of the day was public, praising or shaming a person was an effective use of the rhetorical techniques available to promote social control. Chieftains to commoners could be shamed, so it had the ability to preserve the peace and promote acceptable and honourable conduct while deterring antisocial behaviour.

.

Chapter 5

THE RHETORIC OF CIVIC BONDS
AND SHAME STRUCTURES

> A man should not hold on to the ale-cup,
> But drink moderately from it.
>
> *The Hávamál* (Sayings of the High One)[1]

Introduction

Norse Civic Rhetoric relied heavily on *hóf* to keep the peace and make governing possible. As shown in several sagas and historical documents, *hóf*
allowed small communities to work out civic governing in places where
strong central bureaucracies did not exist. Since medieval Scandinavia was
a praise and shame culture, civic rhetorical involvement helped regulate a
functioning society. Scandinavian civic rhetoric relied heavily on public webs
of engagement. The relationships were reciprocal so that each relationship
would require both parties to think about how they needed to maintain
them for societal stability, and more locally for their families to keep and
nurture relationships. These webs of engagement ranged from household
goði–bóndi relationships, friendships, and family structures, which were
encouraged to stabilize the local community through reasonable actions and
transactions while avoiding any hint of shame to the concerned parties.

Goði–Bóndi Relationship

The rhetoric surrounding the *goði–bóndi* relationship was based on moderation, reasonableness, and reciprocity. *Goði* (pl. *goðar*) were landholders who ran farmsteads in Iceland. Each *goði* had retainers who were small
farmers in their districts and farmhands who worked the main farm. Free
farmers (sing. *bóndi*, pl. *bœndr*) who had sufficient lands and wealth would
often attach to a wealthier landowner in a loose relationship for support.
The wealthier landowner promised to help the *bóndi* in local disputes and
in times of trouble. The *bóndi* promised to support the *goði* in court cases
and local troubles. *The Ljósvetninga Saga* relates an occurrence where a *goði*
named Eyjolf address a meeting of the district farmers,

---

1 Qtd. in Page, *Chronicles of the Vikings*, 142.

"As you well know, I am considered your chieftain. I judge it to be the spirit of our relationship that each aids the other in just cases. You should support me against my opponents while I am to be your ally when your needs require it." People thought that this was right and proper.[2]

"Þat mun ýðr kunnigt, at ek em kallaðr hǫfðingi yðvarr. Nú þykki mér sem þat muni sannligt kaup með oss, ay hvárir veiti ǫðrum at réttum málum ok at þér styrkið oss til móts við mína ágangsmenn, en ek sé yðvarr liðsinnismaðr í yðrum nauðsynjum." Mǫnnum þótti þetta vel sagt.[3]

While this sounds very feudal in nature—a lord gaining fealty from a subordinate—this simply wasn't the case. The relationship and civic rhetoric of the relationship had to be reciprocal. In the case above, Eyjolf focuses not on his chieftaincy for support, but on the spirit of the relationship of mutual aid. This is an important distinction because of the public nature of the discourse. Backdoor deals weren't being made. This was a public gesture towards reciprocity of chieftain and free farmer. Byock contends that "Ostensibly power flowed into the hands of chieftains, but actually much of it remained in the hands of the obstinate farmers. The *bœndr*, aided by their sons and farmhands, guarded their own rights and interests."[4] While the continental system was hierarchical, based on lords and fealty, the Icelandic societal structure retained a strong vein of independence, mutual cooperation, and reciprocal civic duties. Free farmers even had the ability to make promises to two *goðar* at the same time. If the farmstead was close to two chieftaincies, then it was possible to support two *goðar*. Of course, if the two *goðar* became embroiled in a dispute, then the farmer had to choose which one to support, thus damaging the relationship with and expectations of support from the other.

The *bóndi* had certain expectations of support just as much as the *goði* did. If these expectations were not met, then the *bóndi* was free to withdraw his promise and support from his *goði*; if the *goði* behaved erratically, became too belligerent, or acted unevenly in his dealings, then the *bóndi* could promise support to a more even-natured *goði* living somewhere near his farm. The *goði* had to act reasonably in civic matters to keep his supporters; moreover, the public nature of the relationship would be speculated on. An overbearing *goði* might face public shame for his actions. Reasonableness in tone and deed would help generate support in times of trouble. An erratic *goði* may be powerful for a time, but if his support slowly drained

---

2 Andersson and Miller, *Law and Literature*, 211.

3 *Ljósvetninda Saga*, Íslenzk Fornrit, 71.

4 Byock, *Feud in the Icelandic Saga*, 82.

away because of his unruly civic behaviour, he would lose supplies, support, and wealth. Thus, it was important for the *goði* to maintain civil and proper relations with his *bœndr*. As *Hrafnkel's Saga* points out, after Sam has banished Hrafnkel and taken over his farm and *bœndr*,

> The Thjostarssons advised him to be kind, generous and helpful to his men and to support them in anything they needed.
> "They would be worthless men if they failed to give you loyal support then, whenever you needed it."[5]

> Þjóstarssynir réðu honum þat, at hann skyldi vera blíðr okgóðr fjárins ok gagnsamr sínum mǫnnum, styrktarmaðr hvers, sem hans þurfu við.
> "Þá eru þeir eigi menn, ef þeir fylgja þéreigi vel, hvers sem þú þarft við."[6]

In addition to the pledges of support for the *goði*, a *bóndi* also needed to support the *goði* at quarter courts (*þings*) and the summer court at *þing-vellir* the *Alþing*. *Bœndr* were required to pay a fee to attend the *þings*, so they needed to have enough wealth to do this. Sometimes a generous *goði* paid for some retainers to attend with him to gather more support for a pending legal dispute at a *þing*. At times, several *bœndr* would pool their resources to pay the fee and elect a representative to support their *goði* at the *þing*. This pooling of resources created a show of support from less wealthy farming families in the district. Once the fees had been paid, the *bóndi* became a *þingmaður*, a man supporting his particular *goði* at the law court.

One of the important rhetorical points is that the discourse used between *goði* and *bóndi* had to take on a reasonable tone in keeping the peace on the farmstead and in the district. The *goði* couldn't overreach in his temper or demands, nor could the *bóndi* expect too much from the chieftain. The societal forces worked to make sure both sides received the maximum benefit without incurring any shame in the relationship, which might decrease or eliminate bad behaviour on both sides. The public expectations of proper civic behaviour between *goði* and *bóndi* usually resulted in district-wide stability for the most part and worked to curb the worst instincts of the people in the relationship.

---

5 *Hrafnkel's Saga*, trans. Pálsson, 60.
6 *Hrafnkels saga*, The Icelandic Saga Database.

The Rhetoric of Friendship

The idea of friendship in the sagas does not equate to the modern term, and those who read it as a modern term miss the point of the rhetorical choices involved in a friendship relationship. Friendship ritual bonds helped cement relationships to keep the peace, and it was considered a point of honour by the community to keep and reciprocate friendship bonds.

The Old Norse terms for friendship are *vinfengi* and *vinátta*. These terms don't refer to a loose association based on whether the parties involved liked each other, although the term *vinátta* has connotations of a relationship more likely to involve some affection. The *vinfengi* and *vinátta* are terms denoting allies who are willing to support each other in armed conflicts. This type of relationship is politically motivated and practical for security of a landholder's property, so that the major landholders could find common cause in both land disputes and legal disputes. Byock comments that "*Vinfengi* agreements allowed leaders to achieve the collaboration necessary for social control."[7]

These friendship collaborations are spoken of often in the sagas, but they are not generally looked at in terms of their rhetorical significance by using language instead of force to mitigate violence in the community even though, as Sigurðsson argues "friendship was the most important social bond in Iceland and Norway up to middle of the thirteenth century. It did not only shape the power game, but basically it formed the entire social structure, it was the glue that held society together."[8] While Iceland is serving as exemplar in this discussion due to its surviving written sagas, Sigurðsson's work also shows the close cultural relationship between Iceland, Norway, and Sweden throughout the Middle Ages.

Friendship was reinforced in many ways in the sagas. Feasting, gift-giving, and public oaths of friendship showed the close political bonds of friendship. Sections 40–44 of the *Hávamál* have a series of verses on the benefits of friendship and gift-giving. The advice was to trust in good friends and be reciprocal in the giving and receiving of gifts: "those who give to each other / will ay be friends, / Once they meet half way."[9] Friendship relied on the sharing of material wealth, but also on the sharing of support in rough times.

One of the great tragedies in *Njal's Saga* is that Njal and Gunnar have sworn friendship, and this eventually leads to Njal's burning. The saga

---

7 Byock, *Medieval Iceland*, 130.

8 Sigurðsson, *Viking Friendship*.

9 *The Poetic Edda*, trans. Hollander, 20.

states, "Because of their close friendship, Gunnar and Njal used to take turns at inviting one another to an autumn feast."[10] Later, when Njal's wife, Bergthora, and Gunnar's wife, Hallgerd become embroiled in a feud, Njal and Gunnar do their best to keep the peace through their public friendship. When one of Njal's servants is killed at the behest of Hallgerd, Gunnar offers Njal a self-judgement over the incident—a way of allowing Njal to name the terms to keep the peace. Njal accepts the offer, saying "I know that I am dealing with a man of honour, and I do not want to be the cause of any breach in our friendship."[11] Njal and Gunnar keep their friendship and continue feasting and gift-giving to solidify their friendship and to keep the peace in the district.

Perhaps the clearest example of the ideas of friendship as being a political and reciprocal contract comes near the end of *Njal's Saga* when Gizur and Asgrim are petitioning the various *goði* for support. They ask Snorri what help he intends since he was a friend to Njal. He replies,

> I shall do you this act of friendship since your honour will be wholly at stake. I shall not come to court with you; and if a fight breaks out at the Althing, you must not attack before you are absolutely confident of the result…But if you are forced to give ground, you had better retreat in this direction, for I shall have my men drawn up here in battle array ready to come to your help. If on the other hand your opponents retreat…I shall take it upon myself to bar their way.[12]

> Gera skal ek þér vináttubragð þat, er yður sœmð skal ǫll við liggja. En ekki mun ek til dóma ganga, en ef þér berizk á þingi, þá ráðið ér því at eins á þá, nema þér séð allir sem ǫruggastir… n ef þér verðið forviða, þá munuð þér láta slásk hinget til móts við oss, ðví at ek munhafa fylkt liði mínu hér fyrir ok vera við búinn at veita yðr. En ef hin veg ferr, at þeir láti fyrir, þá er þat ætlan min…Mun ek þat á hendr takask at fylka þar fyrir liði mínu ok verja þeim vígit.[13]

This friendship contract clearly defines the risks that Snorri is willing to take on, and the exact terms of the friendship bond. It also positions Snorri as a potential peacemaker if things go badly for Gizur and Asgrim, and as a potential public ally if things go well for the prosecutors of the burning of Njal and his wife.

---

10 *Njal's Saga*, trans. Magnusson and Pálsson, 97.

11 *Njal's Saga*, trans. Magnusson and Pálsson, 112.

12 *Njal's Saga*, trans. Magnusson and Pálsson, 296–97.

13 *Brennu-Njáls Saga*, Íslenzk Fornrit, 372.

The rhetorical idea of gift-giving and feasting also shows the power balances in society. Njal and Gunnar are on generally equal terms since they reciprocate the feasting and gift-giving, but there are poorer people who couldn't possibly return the favours of friendship in this manner. These feasts and gifts demarcated a line of wealth and power because most couldn't throw large banquets. Yet this power structure led the people to view the *goði* as either worthy of respect by honouring bonds with his retainers, or as stingy and a breaker of vows. The feasting between friends in these cases cemented the *goði's* reputation as a public good friend or a fair-weather friend. These gifts also showed the *vinfengi* that his reputation would not be damaged by association with an honourable and generous *goði*. Civically, befriending a well-liked, generous, and well-behaved *goði* could only help stabilize the social fabric, making the rhetorical acts of feasting and gift-giving a reasonable alliance to enter into.

Female friendships in the sagas are much scarcer and more problematic. Since the sagas are focused mainly on the male figures, women often receive minimal attention from the writers. However, the sagas name the term for female friendship, *vinkona*, and there are a few minor references in the sagas. In the *Laxdæla Saga*, Thorgerd told her son Steinthor that "she wanted to go west to Saurby to see her friend Aud."[14] Scholars are divided on the idea of female friendships. Paul Durrenberger and Gísli Pálsson suggest that female friendships only occurred between highborn women or widows of a higher social class. Durrenberger and Pálsson see these relationships in the same mould as male friendships based on wealth and alliance to help maintain political stability. Yet Natalie M. Van Deusen[15] points out that while references to women's friendships in the sagas may be sparse, scholars can infer that women had wider friendships than the sagas describe. Without using the term, *vinkona*, there are many references to women knowing each other and advocating for a marriage bonding for a friend or a friend's daughter. Since women were often excluded from the political sphere, it makes some sense that their friendships are not often mentioned, as the focus of many sagas in the political problems of *goðar*. Yet, friendship between women seems to work in the background of the sagas to create and maintain *hóf* for the household—women work to help cement marriages, they visit friends to keep alliances, and they form bonds that make their households function better.

---

14 *Laxdæla Saga*, trans. Magnusson and Pálsson, 182.

15 For a great discussion on forms of women's friendship, see Van Deusen, "Sworn Sisterhood?," 52–71.

Shame

Rhetorically, shame was an important part of public life in medieval Scandinavia. Early law codes contain rather interesting examinations of the society's use of codification of shame and the public sphere. Shame is usually categorized as *níð*, a general term of public shame. The early *Gulathing* law code of Norway presents a section on *níð* and *níð*-like behaviour. The law is very exacting and demonstrates the seriousness with which the utterance of a *níð* was taken in medieval Nordic society.

> Nobody is to make a verbal *níð* about another person, nor "timber-*níð*" either. If he becomes known for this and is found guilty of it, his penalty is outlawry. Let him deny it with a six-man oath. Outlawry is the outcome if the oath fails. No one is to make an "exaggeration" (*ýki*) about another or libel.[16]

One who portrayed *níð* publicly was named a *níðingr*, a term of shame and scorn. The Icelandic *Grágás* law code also mentions various *níð*-like behaviours. Besides verbally committing a charge of slander as a way of shaming someone, one's actions could also be considered as *níð*-like, and, lastly, there were material rhetorics to embody *níð*. The law codes describe the use of slandering someone for being *níð* or behaving a manner considered *níð*-like as a serious charge. If someone makes a claim of *níð* against someone, then the person must defend themselves in court or even through combat, because the charge of *níð* is such a serious offense.

The idea of *tunguníð*, or *níð* of the tongue (i.e., spoken *níð*) was the worst possible form of slander someone in medieval Scandinavia could endure. Sørensen argues that "It always conveys contempt, and its purpose is to expel the person concerned from the social community as unworthy."[17] In the form of civic rhetoric, charging someone as having *níð* was tantamount to revoking his membership in the community, which was basically a death sentence. The dishonour of *níð* was civic death, and in small, tight-knit communities of medieval Scandinavia, these types of charges became amplified. Knowledge of the charge would be widespread, and there would be no way of hiding or ignoring the accusation. The only reasonable way to respond to this charge would be through court action or through a strong and violent response. Any other response would be viewed as an acquiescence to the charge, which would result in civic ostracism and a loss of all honour. In a society where aggressive behaviour was given high social standing, any acts of public cowardice or passivity were deemed *níð*.

---

16 Sørensen, *The Unmanly Man*, 15.

17 Sørensen, *The Unmanly Man*, 29.

The Vatnsdæla Saga takes up this point and shows how a man's failure to live up to sworn public oaths can lead to *níð* being levelled against him as a form of public shaming, which would reinforce the civic duty that oath-swearing brings. In *The Vatnsdæla Saga*, Jokul—a rather uneven (*ójafn*) man—enters into a feud with Berg and Finnbogi, who are men of prominent families in the Vatnsdæla district. When Jokul's brother fails to achieve a settlement with Berg, violence seems to be inevitable. However, the men in the district think their *goði* is being unreasonable, so he shames them with the threat of *níð*, reminding them of the public oaths they swore:

> Finnbogi is the most fearless of men; but neither one of us need be spared. Berg, the dog, bent lower when I hit him, so that he fell down. You must now turn up to the duel if you have a man's heart rather than a mare's. And if anyone fails to turn up, then a scorn-pole will be raised against him with this curse—that he will be a coward in the eyes of all men, and will never again share the fellowship of good folk, and will endure the wrath of the gods, and bear the name of a truce-breaker.[18]

> en þat er þó eigi ørvænt, ef þeir Finnbogi berjask, því at hann er inn mesti ofrhugi, en hér er hváriga at spara, sem vér erum; fór Bergr þá lútari, bik-kjan, er ek sló hann, svá at hann fell við, enda kom þú nú til hólmstefnunnar, ef þú hefir heldr manns hug en merar; en ef nǫkkurir koma eigi, þá skal þeim reisa níð með þeim formála, at hann skal vera hvers manns níðingr ok vera hvergi í samlagi góðra manna, hafa goða gremi ok griðniðings nafn.[19]

The idea of *níð* is broken down in many ways in the scope of the sagas. *Níð* dealt with passivity and cowardice in actions. In fact, *the Grágás*, or Grey Goose Laws—a collection of Icelandic Laws—even provide for legal judg-ments or trial by arms if accusations of *níð* are proven unfounded. It was a serious enough offense to have judicial precedent for the charges.

In the *Vatnsdæla saga,* when violence becomes inevitable, Jokul travels to duel with Finnbogi and Berg However, due to weather, Jokul's opponents don't show up. Jokul takes the opportunity to shame Berg and Finnbogi by erecting a *níðstöng*:

> Jokul carved a man's head on the end of the post, and wrote in runes the opening words of the curse, spoken of earlier. Jokul then killed a mare, and they cut it open at the breast, and set it on the pole, and had it face towards Borg.[20]

---

18 "The Saga of the People of Vatnsdal," trans. Wawn, 241–42.

19 *Vatnsdœla Saga*, Íslenzk Fornrit, 88–89.

20 "The Saga of the People of Vatnsdal," trans. Wawn, 243–44.

Jǫkull skar karlshǫfuð á súluendanum ok reist á rúnar með ǫllum þeim formála, sem fyrr var sagðr. Siðan drap Jǫkull meri eina, ok opnuðu hana hjá
brjóstinu ok fœrðu á súluna ok létu horfa heim á Borg.[21]

Moreover, since public shaming for cowardice or unmanly acts was demean-
ing and open for public airing, a person who was wronged could make an
accusation by carving a *tréníð*. This type of *níð* was an effigy carved from
wood that depicted the accused of having sex with another man or with an
animal, usually from the accused man's farm. It was set in the road or public
place near the accused's residence so all the townsfolk could see it.

In *Gísli the Outlaw's Saga*, (*Gísla Saga Súrssonar*), Gísli and Bard fail to
show up on time to a duel. After waiting three days for them, Skeggi and
Thorkel decided to shame them by creating a *tréníð*.

Skeggi had come to the isle and staked out the lists for Bard, and laid down
the law of the combat, and after all saw neither him nor any one to fight on
the isle in his stead. There was a man named Fox, who was Skeggi's Smith;
and Skeggi bade Fox to carve likenesses of Gisli and Bard: "And see," he said,
"that one stands just behind the back of the other, and this laughingstock
shall stand for aye to put them to shame."[22]

Skeggi kom til hólmsins ok segir upp hólmgǫngulǫg ok haslar vǫll Kolbirni
ok sér eigi hann þar kominn né þann, er gangi á hólminn fyrir hann.Refr hét
maðr, er var smiðr Skeggja. Hann bað, at Refr skyldi gera mannlíkan eptir
Gísla ok Kolbirni, —"ok skal annarr standa aptar en annarr, ok skal níð þat
standa ávallt, þeim til háðungar."[23]

I must make a point here that the idea of *níð* implies that the accused might
break an oath or not live up to a public vow of support for another person.
The term *níðingr* is for a man who has performed such a shameful action and
is either seen doing it or publicly acknowledges it. For instance, a retainer
who publicly refuses to fight to support his *goði*, especially at legal proceedings or other large public gatherings, risks being called a coward and accru-
ing the title of *níðingr*. Gísli, Bard, Finnbogi, and Berg from the examples
above have been publicly shamed through a *níð*. This type of shame had to be
avenged for their reputations and their families' reputations to be cleansed.
A charge of *níð* was made against them, but their actions would prove if they
would be looked upon by the public as *níðingr*. Their subsequent actions (or
lack of actions) would provide the evidence of the charge.

---

21 *Vatnsdœla Saga*, Íslenzk Fornrit, 91.
22 *The Saga of Gisli the Outlaw*, trans. Dasent.
23 *Gísla Saga Súrssonar*, Íslenzk Fornrit, 10.

These terms are rhetorical in the fact that they are persuasive terms. *Níð* and *níðingr* are used by the public and by *goðar* to move and motivate men to action. The symbolism is perhaps the least important here since these terms can literally cause ostracism, exile, and death to the recipient of such terms. Sørensen summarizes the use of *níð* as a social device to compel action: "The purpose of *níð* is to terminate a period of peace or accentuate a breach of the peace and isolate an opponent from society by declaring that he is unworthy to be a member. The man attacked must show that he is fit to remain in the community, by behaving as a man in the system of Norse ethics."[24] To reestablish his standing in the community, the man accused of *níð* usually had to challenge the accuser to trial by arms, thereby publicly proving that he was both honourable and not a coward. If the man accused was successful in combat, then the charges were shown to be false. While the violence of such a trial was the ending gambit for a person accused, the main point is that men would go out of their way to make reasonable public requests and enter into relationships they could live up to. The idea of *níð* was so strong that it acted as a potent social barrier for men to honour their commitments and act for the public good.

The general forms of *níð* were *argr*, *ragr*, and *ergi*. These terms are problematic in definition but have extremely pejorative meanings in Old Norse. These terms have varying connotations to cowardice and passivity. An *argr*, *ragr*, or *ergi*, can mean a coward who ran away from battle, a male sexual bottom, or even a sorcerer's friend or apprentice. A coward might be someone who refuses to fight and shows his cowardice in a public forum—he deserts the shield wall, his comitatus, fails to live by the warrior's code, or fails to honour an oath. The honour of the man is lessened. He has boasted over his cups and has failed to live up to his word. The society shuns him for this. These terms are broadly used, and a lot of implications are found in the sagas for the *níð*. Scholars such as Byock, Jones, and Sørensen believe the references to *níð* in the sagas rely on connotations and context that we simply don't have which would provide a fuller understanding of the cultural condemnation a *níð* would bring.

Two terms used in the *Grágás* to denote sexual crimes related to *níð* are *stroðinn* and *sorðinn*. These two terms are important in understanding offenses to warriors. According to Sørensen, these two terms translate roughly to "one who has sexually been used by another man."[25] The *níð* struc-

---

24 Sørensen, *The Unmanly Man*, 32.
25 Sørensen, *The Unmanly Man*, 17.

ture for shaming shows how the hyper-masculinized culture viewed passive homosexuality. The culture had strict views of masculine passive behaviour.

Beyond the public sphere, Vikings honoured manliness and male dominance in the bedroom. The *Grágás* laws state that a man must dominate during sex. If you were caught with a woman on top, it was a sign of effeminacy. Being a *ragr*, or a bottom to another man, is another type of cowardly shame to the Vikings. The Norse masculine ideal was to be dominant and aggressive, and if a man was perceived to be passive in his prowess in and out of the bedroom, then it was a mark against him which would incur public shame. The major difference in these terms is that *argr*, *ragr*, or *ergi* suggested a person "willing or inclined to play or interested in playing the female part in sexual relations."[26] The culture expected dominant behaviour by the males, and it was a breach of communal behaviour to be anything else.

The terms *argi*, *ragr*, and *ergi* can denote many forms of non-masculine behaviour. Moreover, the terms of *stroðinn* and *sorðinn* belong in the sexual category of *níð*. However, the mythology of the Norse has many instances where these *níð* structures are broken, including certain mythological stories which contain bestiality and cross-dressing by major figures in the Nordic pantheon.

In the *Þrymskviða*, Thor has his magical hammer, *Mjölnir*, stolen by the giant, Þrymr. To get his hammer back, Thor must give the goddess Freya to the giant as a bride. Instead of giving Freya to the giant, Thor and Loki dress up as bride and bridesmaid and attend the "wedding." Thor's odd behaviour as a woman is explained by Loki in various comic scenes in the tale. Finally, Þrymr hands the hammer over to his bride as a wedding present, and Thor reveals himself and smites the giant with *Mjölnir*.

The comedic tone of the piece is unusual, since Thor would have faced a *níð*, and be considered a *níðingr* for the act of cross-dressing. Yet Thor was one of the most beloved gods. So, why would this occur? Some scholars have suggested that this is an older poem and Thor is being publicly shamed because he has been "unmanned" by having his weapon taken. His masculinity is restored, and his shame is taken when he recovers his hammer and slays the thief. In this interpretation, the public shame is a penance. While other scholars have suggested that this tale is a much later tale and is a parody adapted from the continent, the tone and the feel of the piece seem to fit an older understanding of shame.

In the *Prose Edda*, the origin of Odin's eight-legged horse, Sleipnir, is related and portrays similarly *níð*-like behaviours which include both cross-

---

26 Sørensen, *The Unmanly Man*, 18.

dressing and bestiality. After Valhalla was built, the gods were worried there would be an attack. Then, one day, a builder showed up to build a wall around it. He claimed he could build it in three seasons by himself, and if he did, he would get the beautiful goddess Freya, the sun, and the moon. The gods accepted the offer, and the builder asked if he could use his horse to help him haul the stones. Loki convinced the other gods to agree. By the end of the second season, the wall was well along in construction. The builder's horse, Svaðilfari, was capable of moving incredibly large stones, and the gods were worried he would win the wager. They became angry at Loki for convincing them in the first place. Loki was tasked with figuring out a way to stop the builder's progress. So, Loki shape-shifted into a mare and enticed Svaðilfari into chasing him instead of helping the builder finish the work. The builder became angry, and it was revealed he was secretly a giant trying to steal Freya. Thor killed the builder with *Mjölnir*. *The Prose Edda* suggests that Loki was caught by Svaðilfari because the texts states, "But Loki's relations with Svadilfari were such that a while later he gave birth to a colt."[27]

The clear picture is that Loki was *stroðinn* to Svaðilfari. Loki was always suspect among the gods, so his shame in this instance may be felt to be deserved. He was a trickster, a friend to giants, and the person who had Baldr killed. Yet the terms used are not as judgmental as the social functions of *níð* suggest.

Finally, a *níð* could also be thrown as an accusation of being a sorcerer's friend or apprentice. Sorcery was considered a passive way to kill or bring sickness. Rather than face his opponent in violent combat, a sorcerer cast the spell, which was an act of cowardice. Poisonings and mysterious illnesses could be considered sorcery since they killed passively and from afar. A sorcerer was a coward for killing in secret and not publicly and aggressively, as was more appropriate in Norse society.

For the *níðingr*, rhetoric proved incredibly damaging to their reputations. The poets would often insult the *níðingr* publicly. The root of the modern English word "scold" comes from the Old Norse word skald or poet. The poet had the ultimate responsibility to rhetorically put offenders into their place. The poets would wait until they were performing in front of retainers, warriors, other chieftains, and the assembled households to publicly shame the offenders deemed *níðingr*.

The Saga of Cormac the Skald uses this rhetorical stance to insult men who have been deemed in the story to lack the *drengskapr*, or honour. For instance, Thorvard didn't like Cormac, and he paid a beggar to sing a song shaming Steingard as a witch. Then, he blamed Cormac for the creation of

---

27 *The Prose Edda*, trans. Byock, 52.

the song. Culturally, the skalds could write songs of shame to entertain and instruct the farm holds. However, this was a libel against Steingard since she wasn't a witch. Cormac's reputation was damaged by this lie, and, thus, his honour was also damaged. Cormac challenged Thorvard to a duel (*holm-gang*) to satisfy and restore Cormac's honour, but Thorvard didn't arrive for the duel. Irritated that Thorvard didn't show up, Cormac decides to make a real verse shaming the man for cowardice.

> "Now," said Cormac, "I bid Thorvard anew to the holmgang, if he can be called in his right mind. Let him be every man's nithing if he come not!" and then he made this song:

> "The nithing shall silence me never
> Though now for their shame they attack me,
> But the wit of the Skald is my weapon,
> And the wine of the gods will uphold me.
> And this they shall feel in its fulness;
> Here my fame has its birth and beginning;
> And the stout spears of battle shall see it,
> If I 'scape from their hands with my life."

> Then the brothers set on foot a law-suit against him for libel. Cormac's kins-men backed him up to answer it, and he would let no terms be made, saying that they deserved the shame put upon them, and no honour; he was not unready to meet them, unless they played him false. Thorvard had not come to the holmgang when he had been challenged, and therefore the shame had fallen of itself upon him and his, and they must put up with it.[28]

> Kormákr mælti: "Nú býð ek Þorvarði af nýju
> holmgǫngu. Verði hann hvers manns níðingr,
> ef hann kemr eigi, ef hann telsk hugar síns eigandi."
> Ok þá kvað Kormákr vísu: Skulut níðingar neyða, nú
> emk sóttr um gjǫf dóttur, upp held ek Gauta
> gildi, gǫgnum, mik til þagnar þat
> nu þróttar víttir þropregns stafir fregna, byrjak
> frægð, nema fjǫrvi félmiðlendr
> mik véli. Þá búa þeir brǿðr mál til á hendr Kormáki um
> níð. Frændr Kormáks halda upp svǫrum. Hann vill engi
> boð bjóða láta. Kvað þá níðs verða, en eigi sóma.
> Ok kvazk Kormákr ekki við þeim vanbúinn, útan þeir svíki
> hann. Þorvarðr hafði eigi sótt holmstefnu þá, er Kormákr
> bauð honum, sagði Kormákr sjalffellt níð á þá ok
> þeim makligt at þola slíkt níð.[29]

---

28 *The Saga of Cormac the Skald*, trans. Collingwood and Stefansson.

29 AM 132 fol. (120vb.21–129rb.7): *Kormáks saga.*

Cormac's rhetorical strategy of shaming Thorvard for cowardice is poetic justice. By attempting to shame Cormac and his craft, Thorvard fell victim to the art of skaldic poetry. This scene from *The Saga of Cormac* once again shows shame culture and the rhetoric surrounding it were sewn into the fabric of Norse society. Values of honourable conduct were public and open for public commentary. By not appearing for the duel, Cormac has labelled Thorvard as a *níðingr*—he is not a man who needs reinforcement of a code of right conduct, but Thorvard is now a man who has failed to live up to that social contract. The accusation has become a failed deed, and, so, Thorvard is now labelled a coward publicly.

Additionally, one could respond to a call for shame by erecting a *níðstöng*, or a *níð*-pole, as done by Jokul to Finnbogi and Berg. A *níðstöng* is a pole raised on another's property which was set on top with the head of a slaughtered animal, usually a horse, and carved with runes which list the name of the offender and the crime he is accused of. The pole acts as a public form of shame. The Norse use of such public displays were intended to regulate honour and denigrate shameful activities, as clearly shown in the sagas. For instance, in *Egil's Saga*,

> When their sails were hoisted, Egil went back to the island.
> He took a hazel pole in his hand and went to the edge of a rock facing inland. Then he took a horse's head and put it on the end of the pole.
> Afterwards he made an invocation saying, "Here I set up this scorn-pole and turn its scorn upon King Eirik and Queen Gunnhild"—then he turned the horse's head to face land—"and I turn its scorn upon the nature spirits that inhabit this land, sending them all astray so that none of them will find its resting-place by chance or design until they have driven King Eirik and Queen Gunnhild from this land."
> Then he thrust the pole into a cleft in the rock and left it to stand there. He turned the head towards the land and carved the whole invocation in runes on the pole.[30]

> Búast þeir til at sigla, ok er þeir váru seglbúnir, gekk Egill upp í eyna. Hann tók í hönd sér heslistöng ok gekk á bergsnös nökkura, þá er vissi til lands inn. Þá tók hann hrosshöfuð ok setti upp á stöngina.
> Síðan veitti hann formála ok mælti svá: "Hér set ek upp níðstöng, ok sný ek þessu níði á hönd Eiríki konungi ok Gunnhildi dróttningu"— hann sneri hrosshöfðinu inn á land— "sný ek þessu níði á landvættir þær, er land þetta byggva, svá at allar fari þær villar vega, engi hendi né hitti sitt inni, fyrr en þær reka Eirík konung ok Gunnhildi ór landi."

---

30 *Egil's Saga*, trans. Scudder, 106.

Síðan skýtr hann stönginni niðr í bjargrifu ok lét þar standa. Hann sneri ok höfðinu inn á land, en hann reist rúnar á stöngina, ok segja þær formála þenna allan.[31]

In this example, the shame is heaped upon the king and queen. Not only did Egil seek to publicly shame them, but he also carved runes upon the pole, so people could read the curse. Rhetorically, the *níðstöng* functions as a symbol showing public scorn for actions. Egil, in this instance, is shaming Eirik and Gunnhild for seizing property—specifically land—belonging to Egil.

The rhetorical shaming with the *níðstöng* has perhaps never gone out of style in Scandinavia. According to the Icelandic news site, *Visir*, in 2006, a man claiming to be in the direct descent from Egil Skallagrimsson used a *níðstöng* to shame a neighbour for accidently killing his dog. The man who created the pole was arrested since the authorities considered the *níðstöng* as a death threat. Similarly, a man used a *níðstöng* adorned with sheep's heads in Norway as part of an election protest. Another instance in Iceland occurred in 2016, when the Icelandic Prime Minister was indicted for corruption in the Panama Papers scandal. Several protesters stood in front of the *Alþingi* with a *níðstöng* that had a horse skull and dried codfish among them. These instances show the rhetorical significance of the *níð* shaming to this day. Using the historical basis for the shame culture throughout Scandinavia, the symbolic action of the pole represents accusations against people who have broken codes of conduct and are being publicly shamed to force a course of action. The sagas' messages of correct public action are still in the public imagination today, and the *níðstöng* still carries rhetorical weight— even after almost a thousand years.

Goading

In the sagas, not everyone had access to the court system or to modes of policing civic obligation. Since the masculine world of the medieval Scandinavians excluded women and often did not address intrafamily squabbles, another method of advocacy and resolution was needed. People without direct legal recourse (e.g. women, bondsmen [ON *bóndi*], and retainers) needed a method of persuasion to motivate the men in charge who could act in this society. Given the circumstances of the civic and legal structure in medieval Scandinavia, goading a person to act in the family/farm/district's best interest was a reasonable move for the goader. If the goader could successfully point out that the male being goaded might incur shame upon him

---

31 | *Egils Saga*, The Icelandic Saga Database.

or the family, then the male might be inclined to act at the behest of the goader for reasons of honour and saving face among his retainers. Some scholars suggest that goading only served as a literary device, but William Ian Miller suggests it is too critical in the scope of the Nordic society to be just a literary device: "Some would say the vengeance minded woman was nothing more than a literary commonplace...But if she was a commonplace, it is indeed remarkable how much social and psychological sense her role made."[32]

Miller's observation rings true when thinking about the reasonableness of a goader's position. A person without recourse under the legal system would need other avenues of recourse. Miller further points out, "What was common to all inciters was not their sex but their dependence on the men they incited."[33] Since one of the duties of wives and retainers was to maintain the reputation of their family or farmstead, then the social sense of goading becomes clear. The threat of shame was often enough to move men to action is settings where the power structures excluded all from taking part in the discussions outside the farmsteads. To maintain one's reputation and honour and avoid shame in the district, goading becomes a rhetorical device which people outside the *þing* system could use to move reluctant men—those who could actively repair or save their reputation—to action. This goading is a rhetorical exercise in reminding the men in charge that without action, shame will result for them, the family, and the farm.

Servants, perhaps the lowest rung on the hierarchy in the Nordic farmstead (only above slaves) also goaded the landowners to action. *The Heiðarviga Saga*, or *The Story of the Heath Slayings*, which is one of the earliest and most fragmentary of the Icelandic sagas, contains an early reference to a servant goading his landholder to action. Bardi's brother Hall is killed, but Bardi sees the problem of taking vengeance. However, one of his servants, Thord the Fox, sees that Bardi's reputation will suffer if he doesn't take action, which would also endanger to the farm. Thord goads him on thus,

> Bardi and his brethren were without, when the workingmen came, and they greeted them well. They had their work-tools with them, and Thord the Fox was dragging his scythe behind him.
> Quoth Bardi: "Now Draggeth the Fox his brush behind him."

---

32 Miller, *Bloodtaking and Peacemaking*, 212.

33 Miller, *Bloodtaking and Peacemaking*, 212.

"So it is," saith Thord, "that I drag my brush behind me, and cock it up but little or nought; but this my mind bodes me, that thou will thy brush very long or ever thou avenge Hall thy brother.[34]

Barði var úti og þeir bræður er þeir komu heim verkmennirnir. Heilsuðu þeir þeim vel. Höfðu þeir með sér verksfæri sín og dregur Þórður melrakki eftir sér ljáorf sitt.

Barði mælti: "Dregur Melrakki eftir sér halann sinn nú."

"Svo er," segir hann Þórður, "að eg dreg eftir mér halann minn og ber eg lítt upp eða ekki. En þess varir mig að þú dragir þinn hala mjög lengi áður þú hefnir Halls bróður þíns."[35]

Thord is used in the saga to show that the inaction displayed by Bardi is unwanted and unhelpful for making the farm function effectively. Thord the Fox is holding up a mirror to Bardi to illustrate the lack of action. Later in the sequence,

Now he [Bardi] bade Thord to this, because the wether [*sic*] was worse to catch than other sheep, and swifter withal. "Now further to-morrow shalt thou go to Ambardale, and fetch home the five-year-old ox which we have there, and slaughter him, and bring all the carcass south to Burg on Saturday. Great is the work, but if thou win it not, then shalt thou try which of us bears the brush most cocked thenceforward."

Thord answered and said that often he heard his big threats; and thereof he is nowise blate.[36]

því vísaði hann honum til þess að hann var verra að henda en aðra sauði og var hann skjótari - "nú skaltu og á morgun sækja í Ambáttardal yxin fimm vetra gamalt er vér eigum og drepa af og færa slátrið allt til Borgar suður laugardag. Verkið er mikið en ef ei er unnið þá muntu reyna hvor halann sinn ber brattara þaðan frá."

Þórður svarar og kveðst oft hafa heyrt hót hans digur og blotnar hann ei við.[37]

Since Thord was purposefully slacking in his work duties, Bardi threatens him with violence if he doesn't complete the task assigned. However, Thord publicly shames him by saying Bardi's boasts are often grand but seldom lived up to. The scene ends with Bardi riding off the farm, shamed into action by the servant. This early scene from *The Heiðarviga Saga* serves to

---

34 *The Story of the Heath Slayings*, trans. Morris and Magnusson, 20.

35 *Heiðarvíga Saga.*

36 The Story of the Heath Slayings, trans. Morris and Magnusson, 21.

37 *Heiðarvíga Saga.*

illustrate the power of rhetorical shaming which cut across levels of society. But this is not the only evidence of this type of rhetorical ploy from servants on the farm.

In *Hrafnkel's Saga*, a servant woman who was washing clothes happened to see Eyvind, the brother of a man who had Hrafnkel outlawed and seized his property. Hrafnkel moved east and started fresh, and he often saw the man who took his lands but did nothing about it. The washer-woman ran to Hrafnkel and said, "The old saying is true enough, 'The older a man, the feebler.' The honour a man's given early in life isn't worth much if he has to give it all up in disgrace, and he hasn't the courage to fight for his rights ever again. It's a peculiar thing indeed to happen to those who were once thought brave."[38] At the woman's goading, Hrafnkel and his retainers armed themselves and pursued Eyvind.

Þingmenn also goaded their *goði* (chieftain) to an action by bringing up the shame of inaction. In the *Ljósvetninga Saga*, Einar chides the proud and indulgent Gudmund: "You value no one's opinion but your own in this case, but it may be that your success will fall short of your ambition."[39] When the charges are filed against Akra-Thorir for a failure to produce some seized property, Thorir Helgason says, "There isn't much help to be expected from you; it always turns out that you knuckle under to Gudmund."[40] Later, Isolf approaches one of Gudmund's sons, Eyjolf, and flatly states, "My business is not calculated to enhance your honour, but still, we thingmen look to you for support. We think that the action of the Fnjoskadalers is a blatant disgrace... It will be considered you are losing status unless, of course, men more distinguished than you should intervene."[41] In these examples, the *goðar* are shamed for not using the counsel of their retainers. Advice is important because it helps build consensus on a prudent course of action which could otherwise end in violence against the entire retinue of the chieftain. Moreover, the honour of the household and farmstead is threatened with public shame and lack of honour.

But perhaps the most common form of goading to be found in the sagas is that of the wife goading her *goði* husband or her sons to action. It must be noted that goading is always a public event. An audience must be there to hear the goading and bring the public nature of the shame culture to bear upon the recipient. In these instances, a woman who was forbidden

38 *Hrafnkel's Saga*, trans. Pálsson, 63–64.

39 Andersson and Miller, *Law and Literature*, 174.

40 Andersson and Miller, *Law and Literature*, 174.

41 Andersson and Miller, *Law and Literature*, 206.

by society from taking vengeance on her own would wait for an assembly of the *goði*'s retainers, warriors, and perhaps other goðar from nearby farms to insult her lord for failing to act in the best interests of society. It could have been for failing to act to bring a legal case against a killing, or it could have been failing to seek blood feud against another *goði* for the slaying of a relative. A scene from *The Íslendinga Saga* illustrates the importance of the public nature of the goading: "Alf...reminded Brand that Thoralf had been actively involved in the killing of Kalf and his son Guttorm. But Brand's wife Jorunn would not join in [the discussion]. She was the daughter of Kalf. *And the General view was that she had not goaded Brand."*[42]

In *The Saga of the People of Laxardal*, Thorgerd Egilsdottir goads her other sons to attack a man named Bolli for killing Kjartan, her son and their brother. As they ride past Bolli's farmstead, she asks her sons to whom the farm belongs, and says:

> What I do know...is that here lives Bolli, your brother's slayer, and not a shred of resemblance do you bear to your great ancestors since you won't avenge a brother the likes of Kjartan. Never would your grandfather Egil have acted like this, and it grieves me to have such spineless sons. You would have made your father better daughters, to be married off, than sons. It shows the truth of the saying, Halldor, that 'every kin has its coward'. I see only too well now that fathering such sons was Olaf's greatest failing...I made the journey mainly to remind you of what you seem to have forgotten.
>
> Halldor then answered, 'You're the last person we could blame, Mother, if it did slip from our minds.
>
> Halldor had little else to say, although his hatred for Bolli swelled.[43]

> "Veit ek at vísu," segir hon, "at hér býr Bolli, bróðurbani yðvarr, ok furðu ólíkir urðu þér yðrum frændum gǫfgum, er þér vilið eigi hefna þvílíks bróður, sem Kjartan var, ok eigi myndi svá gera Egill, móðurfaðir yðvarr, ok er illt at eiga dáðlausa sonu; ok víst ætla ek yðr til þess betr fellda, at þér værið dœtr fǫður yðvars ok værið giptar. Kemr hér at því, Halldórr, sem mælt er, at einn er auðkvisi ættar hverrar, ok sú er mér auðsæst ógipta Óláfs, at honum glapðisk svá mjǫk sonaeignin; kveð ek þik af því at þessu, Halldórr," segir hon, "at þú þykkisk mest fyrir yðr brœðrum. Nú munu vér aptr snúa, ok var þetta ørendit mest, at minna yðr á þetta, ef þér mynðið eigi áðr."
>
> Þá svarar Halldórr: "Ekki munu vér þér þat kenna, móðir, þótt oss líði ór hug þetta."
>
> Halldórr svarar hér fá um, ok þó þrútnaði honum mjǫk móðr til Bolla.[44]

---

42 Miller, *Bloodtaking and Peacemaking*, 213, emphasis in Miller.

43 "The Saga of the People of Laxardal," trans. Kunz, 377.

44 *Laxdæla Saga*, Íslenzk Fornrit, 162.

Impugning her sons' manhood and comparing them to the glory and masculinity of the past draws on a common trope in the sagas. Thorgerd shows
that public declarations of cowardice are effective rhetorical means to persuade her sons to take action.

Similarly, in *Eyrbyggja Saga*, when Thorbjorn goes to Thorarin's farm
without warrant to accuse Thorarin of stealing horses, Thorarin backs
down. When Thorarin's mother sees this, she rushes forward, exclaiming,

> "It's true what they say about you, Thorarin," she said. "You're more like a
> woman than a man, putting up as you do with all Thorbjorn's insults. I can't
> think whatever I did to have a son like you."
>
> ...
>
> "I'm not standing around here any longer," said Thorarin, and rushed for-
> ward with his men.[45]

> Þá gekk Geirríðr út í dyrrnar ok sá, hvat er títt var, ok mælti: "Ofsatt er þat,
> er mælt er, at meir hefir þú, Þórbirni digra hverja skǫmm, ok eigi veit ek, hví
> ek á slíkan son."
>
> ...
>
> Þórarinn svarar: "Eigi nenni ek nú lengr hér at standa." Eptir þetta hlaupa
> þeir Þórarinn út ok vilja hleypa up dóminum.[46]

Additionally, In the *Laxdæla Saga*, Gudrun goads her husband and brothers
to take vengeance on Kjartan over a broken oath and a public loss of face for
her family.

> Gudrun said, "you would have had just the right temper if you had been
> peasants' daughters—you do nothing about anything, whether good or bad.
> Despite all of the disgrace and the dishonour that Kjartan has done to you,
> you lose no sleep over it even when he rides past your door with only a sin-
> gle companion. Men like you have the memory of hogs. It's obviously futile
> to hope that you will ever dare to attack Kjartan at home if you haven't the
> nerve to face him now when he is travelling with only one or two compan-
> ions. You just sit at home pretending to be men, and there are always too
> many of you about."
>
> Ospak said she was making too much of this, but admitted that it was dif-
> ficult to argue against her. He jumped out of bed at once and dressed, as did
> all the brothers one after another; then they made ready to lay an ambush
> for Kjartan.

---

45 *Eyrbyggja Saga*, trans. Pálsson and Edwards, 51.

46 *Eyrbyggja Saga*, Íslenzk Fornrit, 36.

Gudrun now asked Bolli to go with them. Bolli said it would not be right for him to do that because of his kinship with Kjartan, and he recalled how lovingly Olaf had brought him up.

"That's perfectly true," said Gudrun. "But you don't have the luck to be able to please everybody; and if you refuse this journey, it will be the end of our marriage."

And at Gudrun's promptings, Bolli remembered all his resentment against Kjartan, and he armed himself quickly.[47]

Guðrún mælti: "Gott skaplyndi hefði þér fengit, ef þér værið dœtr einshvers bónda ok láta hvárki at yðr verða gagn né mein; en slíka svívirðing ok skǫmm, sem Kjartan hefir yðr gǫrt, þá sofi þér eigi at minna, at hann ríði hér hjá garði við annan mann, ok hafa slíkir menn mikit svínsminni; þykki mér ok rekin ván, at þér þorið Kjartan heim at sœkja, ef þér þorið eigi at finna hann nú , er hann ferr við annan mann eða þriðja, en þér sitið heima ok látið vænliga ok eruð æ hǫlzti margir."

Óspakr kvað hana mikit af taka, en vera illt til mótmæla, ok spratt hann upp þegar ok klæddisk, ok hverr þeira brœðra at ǫðrum. Síðan bjuggusk þeir at sitja fyrir Kjartani.

Þá bað Guðrún Bolla til ferðar með þeim. Bolli kvað sér eigi sama fyrir frændsemis sakar við Kjartan ok tjáði, hversu ástsamliga Óláfr hafði hann upp fœddan.

Guðrún svarar: "Satt segir þú þat, en eigi muntu bera giptu til at gera svá, at ǫllum þykki vel, ok mun lokit okkrum samfǫrum, ef þú skersk undan fǫrinni."

Ok við fortǫlur Guðrúnar miklaði Bolli fyrir sér fjándskap allan á hendr Kjartani ok sakar ok vápnaðisk siðan skjótt, ok urðu níu saman.[48]

From these examples it is clear that one of the rhetorical moves for a woman in medieval Scandinavia was to goad men into action. By attacking the men in ways that make them appear publicly weak or ineffective, the women in these examples were able to move men to action. These examples also hint at the troubles inherent in the division of roles inside and outside the household. In the outer world, men may have constraints put on them to save face or be motivated not to take action, for fear of the shame they would face when, for example, they would take vengeance on a family member and breaking societal taboos on kin-slaying. On the farmstead, the woman's role is to defend the home and reputation of the family. If an event occurs, it is her duty to defend the reputation of the homestead and to rouse her male relatives to the action she cannot undertake.

---

47 *Laxdæla Saga*, trans. Magnusson and Pálsson, 172.

48 *Laxdæla Saga*, Íslenzk Fornrit, 150.

Andersson and Miller point out that "Goading, needling, and insinuating suggestion simply seem to be key elements in the rhetoric of persuasion in the culture, available to those who need to persuade. The art of persuasion, although useful to all, is especially so to those who must act with others or through others."[49] Rather than consider goading simply a literary common-place, then, it may be better and more effective to consider the three rhetorical *topoi* suggested by these examples. First, there is a *topos* in which the servants and retainers attempt to shame their *goði* into action by attacking his reputation among the servants and retainers. The public values they held are evident through their method of shaming language. The workers in the village and farmstead valued a strong work ethic and a responsive *goði*. When the *goði* failed to uphold these values, the retainers could goad him to action by reminding him of the public values to save face among his retainers. The audience had to be aware of the values of the day to understand this rhetorical ploy to move the *goði* to action.

The second *topos* would be that of *þingmenn* goading their chieftain to action. *Goðar* had well defined roles in terms of actions with their *þingmenn*, and if a *goði* failed to act—or if he acted improperly—it would be a reasonable ploy to bring the *goði* back into the realm of acceptable behaviour by goading. When the *þingmenn* entered a relationship with a *goði*, there would be an expectation of help and support from the more powerful *goði*, either with force or legal help. Consequently, if the retainer believed the *goði* to be acting inappropriately, society would expect goading to remind the *goði* of the oaths sworn for mutual help.

The third type of goading *topos* was between a woman and her husband or sons. The family dynamic plays a crucial part here since the woman's role was to maintain her family and farm. This responsibility included looking after the reputation and safety of the farms. In medieval Scandinavia, it was common for women to manage farmsteads for long periods if her husband was off at a *þing* or if he went off raiding. The goading here is meant to ensure the reputation and safety of the farmstead and family. Because women were generally forbidden from taking an active role in legal conflict and vengeance taking, they logically looked for the intermediary who had the power to act publicly. The goading in these cases attacked the masculinity and virile prowess of the *goði* as well as his bravery or the bravery of his sons. Cowardly actions could bring about raids on the farmstead when the men were away, so it was important to broadcast a public display of strength to the region around the farm. The goading woman in the sagas was not por-

---

49 Andersson, and Miller, *Law and Literature*, 20.

trayed as shrewish. Rather, the goader was expected to perform these duties and remind her husbands and sons in a public manner of the duties expected of them to maintain their household. This course of action would have been considered a reasonable approach for a caring wife and mother to take.

Conclusion

The Norse idea of *hóf*, or reasonableness, plays an important part in examining the civic rhetoric of the medieval Scandinavians. They preferred to resolve disputes peacefully, despite the honour associated with violence. The systems discussed here developed as a means to keep the peace, and if people were considered *óhóf*, or unreasonable, they gained a black mark in public opinion. To be labelled as *ójafnaðarmaðr*, or an unjust or overbearing man, was considered a stern public rebuke in the north. It could lead to public shaming or act as a prelude to violence since the average citizen was supposed to adopt a stance of reasonableness.

People mentioned in the sagas are often categorized in terms of their reasonableness. Relationships, such as friendships, are often categorized in terms of their even-handedness and reasonableness. As will be evidenced further later in this book, people who are reasonable will take and make settlements to keep the peace and maintain civic order while the villains are often men and women who are unreasonable. The stain of looking unreasonable in a society built on the premise of personal honour and reputation could have long and lasting repercussions.

Chapter 6

"LOUD APPROVAL AT THE LAW ROCK"

THE NORDIC LEGAL TRADITION

"With laws shall our land be built up
but with lawlessness laid waste."

Njáls Saga[1]

TO CLAIM THAT the medieval Norse had an incredibly legal mindset would not be an understatement. The sagas, as cultural artifacts, often suggest that the rule of law is extremely important in the makeup of their society. The sagas show court cases, lawyers as a profession, rhetorical training of lawyers, and the spaces of legal rhetoric. This information from the sagas is reinforced by archaeological and historical research which looks at the pre-eminence of law as a cultural factor. In fact, our modern word "law" is derived from the Old Norse *lög*.[2] Variant words such as law, lawman, outlaw, bylaw, etc. all derive from the Old Norse root word, not the Latin, French, or the continental jurist traditions from which many of our legal terms were taken. Furthermore, after England was conquered by the Danish "Great Heathen Army" in 865, the northern and eastern parts of England were partitioned off into a Danish controlled area. Rather than call this area a heathendom, the English term was Dane-law—a place where Danish law and customs prevailed. Even this historical reference to a Viking invasion is coupled with their profound respect for a law code. The medieval Scandinavians had developed a legal rhetoric based on the concept of *hóf* and reasonable dealings. Nordic lawyers had codified techniques and traditions which fit their world of oral traditions and easily transitioned into the vernacular period after the conversion to Christianity. These legal techniques were tested in courts and transmitted from generation to generation through medieval fosterage with trained lawyers.

---

* A portion of this chapter has been published in Lively, "We Must Always Go Fully Armed," 81–96.

1 *Njal's Saga*, trans. Magnusson and Pálsson, 159.

2 *The Oxford English Dictionary* has an interesting discussion and listing of the history and usage of the English word "law" and its derivative forms. Gordon's *An Introduction to Old Norse*, and Byock's *Viking Language 1* and *Viking Language 2* were extremely helpful in researching the language for this chapter.

The legalistic nature of the medieval Nordic people shows a culture centred on legal processes, and scholars who focus on Viking raids and brutality are often studying an aftereffect of such legal processes. Those Norse who were outlawed by a court judgment frequently became raiders feared by the chroniclers. Once exiled, those men were often hired on to mercenary bands or travelled to Norway or Denmark where they could earn a living in martial pursuits and, perhaps, gain enough bounty to placate the families whom they had offended. From close examination of the sagas and historical interpretation, it becomes clear that medieval Scandinavian society is dominated by their legal structure. Thus, these "lawless barbarians" were quite constrained in many ways by the law that governed their day-to-day lives.

An examination of the legal materials that have survived makes it clear that the rhetorical stance of *hóf* is the framework that dominated the legal sphere of medieval Scandinavia. The legal system fit consistently into the civic values of the medieval Scandinavians, and the reasonableness of their rhetoric created legal structures to help keep the peace and make sure no party involved lost face. As with their civic rhetoric, the legal cases needed to be public and open for all to see. This chapter explores the places of legal rhetoric, rhetorical education and training, and advocacy and mediation, with the support of textual examples of the efforts to use reasonableness to maintain peace through the legal process.

The Rhetoric of Legal Space

Hawhee and Olson's "Pan-Historiography" emphasizes that, in order to examine cultural trends, it is important to look at a broad frame of space and time and then to focus in on specific examples to illustrate the broad picture.[3] Using this general-to-particular focus can help to explain the importance of legal proceedings and the spaces these events occupied in medieval Norse society. Hawhee and Olson argue that "writing histories whose temporal scope extends well beyond the span of individual generations…to studies that leap across geographic space, tracking important activities, terms, movements, or practices as they travel with trade, with global expansion."[4] To truly understand the legal rhetoric of the medieval Nordic peoples, one must first understand the cultural and the geographical contexts in which this rhetoric was embedded. For the Vikings, this legal space was associated

---

3 Hawhee and Olson, "Pan-Historiography," 90–105.

4 Hawhee and Olson, "Pan-Historiography," 90.

with place, specifically *þings*[5] (lit. "assembly" in *Old Norse*). In the Germanic tradition, all legal and legislative assemblies took place outside under the open sky. Tacitus discusses the idea of the court assembly in *Germania*.

> When the assembled crowd is ready, they take their seats, carrying arms. Silence is commanded by the priests, who have on these occasions the right to enforce obedience. Then the king or the chiefs are heard in accordance with each one's age, nobility, military distinction, or eloquence. The power of persuasion counts for more than the right to give orders.[6]

At the *þings*, legislative business was conducted and court cases were heard by a group of appointed judges. The concept of an assembly (a *þing*) is a very old idea, and wherever Nordic people settled, they established *þings*. These assemblies were held beneath the open sky, sometimes set in a grouping of stones, and public for everyone to see.

The portrayal of Viking *þings* in the sagas provide a way to examine their legal structure. Gwynn Jones argues that "It was long held that a substantial body of custom and law could be recovered from saga sources, and indeed it can, but what is now very much in dispute is how reliable was the information transmitted."[7] According to Jones, the writing of the sagas was done in the thirteenth and fourteenth centuries and the court cases from the sagas thus show a later representation of law. In light of modern scholarship we need to ask whether the fundamentals of the structure, pleading, and laws are all that different from saga times. Many medieval practices remained somewhat static for long periods of time, from textiles to farming to building, so would the law shown here be very different? Modern scholarship suggests not.[8]

Ari Thorgillson chronicles the early genesis of the legal codes in *The Book of the Icelanders*

> The first summer that Bergthor spoke the law, an innovation was made that our law should be written down in a book at the home of Hafliði Másson the following winter at the dictation and with the guidance of Hafliði and Bergþórr, as well as of other wise men appointed for this task. They were to make new provisions in the law in all cases where these seemed to them better than the old laws. These were to be proclaimed the next summer in

---

5 The thorn (þ) in Old Norse represented a modern unvoiced English "th" sound, IPA [θ].

6 Tacitus, *Agricola and Germania*, 43.

7 Jones, *History of the Vikings*, 345.

8 See, for example, Winroth, *The Age of the Vikings*, Jesch, *The Viking Diaspora*, and Price, *Children of Ash and Elm*.

the Law Council, and all those were to be kept which a majority of people did not oppose.[9]

et fyrsta sumar, es Bergþórr sagþi lög upp, vas nýmæli þat gørt,at lög ór scylldi scriva á bóc at Hafliþa Mós-sonar of vetrenn epter at sögo oc umbráþi þeira Bergþórs oc annara spacra manna, þeira es til þess výro tecner. scylldu þeir gørva nýmæli þau öll í lögom, es þeim litisc þau betri, an en forno lög. scylldi þau segja upp et næsta sumar epter í lögrétto, oc þau öll hallda, es enn meiri hlutr manna mælti þá eigi gegn.[10]

Since Ari was writing in 1117–1118, this makes his accounts fairly close to the actual time of the events. Furthermore, Ari gained this information from talking to witnesses to events. A man named Teitr is often mentioned as a source, and Ari even mentions interviews with people who had travelled to both Greenland and America (Vinland). Ari chronicles the settling of Iceland and the conversion to Christianity in Iceland, which I will discuss further in the following chapter. Archaeologists' and historians' findings can help demonstrate that much of what Ari chronicled was true. For instance, settlements have been found in Greenland and Nova Scotia as evidence that Vikings were there. Additionally, Ari claims that Iceland was completely settled in sixty years. Recent archaeological studies back up this claim. If so many of Ari's claims are true, then we must consider his rendering of legal tradition taken from primary sources as probably true—or at least largely so—as well.

This is not to say that Icelandic law is the final word when looking at the medieval Scandinavian law codes. However, it does provide a baseline for looking at the topic as a whole. A majority of the Icelanders came from Norway during the *landnáma* (the land-taking) during the settlement period, circa 870–930. The legal codes and *þings* were carried from the mainland to Iceland during the settlement. Norway, for example, has its own legal codes as represented in the *Gulaþing* and *Frostaþing* laws, which were fairly contemporary with Icelandic law—although these Norwegian laws appear to be rooted in an even earlier legal tradition. The idea that a widespread legal tradition appeared and flourished before the conversion, and before the vernacular period, is important to consider when looking at the legal aspects in the sagas. These legal representations become important representative examples of the broad legal structures in the medieval north. It also explains why the sagas were so well received outside of Iceland. These examples resonated with the audiences on the continent, where those external to Norse

---

9 Thorgilsson, *The Book of the Icelanders*, trans. Grønlie, 12.

10 Thorgilsson, *Íslendingabók*, 18–19.

legal processes could see elements of a shared culture of reasonable decisions in the sagas.

In any case, the lawyers in the sagas are clearly a known and structured class of legal rhetors in the Viking world. The descriptions of *þings* in the Viking world show a broad diaspora of this cultural phenomenon. As with any cultural system, specialists in the area will develop and create language and tradition (i.e., a discourse) for the members of that community. The medieval Nordic lawyers developed this as well. Lawyers were apprenticed to a legal expert to learn the law. This type of inculcation of lawyers gave them the ability to plead cases and also to offer legal advice to those who needed it. There are many examples of lawyers' advice-giving in the sagas. With the descriptions of the legal discourse community, the sagas strongly indicate a legal rhetorical tradition outside of the classical norm.

Olwyn Owen´s book, *Things in the Viking World,*[11] examines the widespread development of *þings* across the Viking diaspora. Based on archaeological findings and linguistic information, *þing* sites appear across the Scandinavian expansion during the early medieval period. Owen's findings show the vast and diverse localities of the *þings*. Norway, Denmark, Iceland, Sweden, Great Britain, Ireland, the Faroe Islands, the Shetland Islands, and Greenland all boast *þing* sites. Due to the vast amount of found sites, the institution of the *þing* is shown to be prevalent in the Viking world.

From the archaeological data, *þings* appeared to be fewer where strong central government existed or where the population had easier access to a court assembly. The Shetlands and Great Britain seem to have many *þing* sites, due to isolated geographical populations and the difficulty of travel to the assemblies, which apparently prompted local communities to develope their own. Even places such as Greenland and Russia have potential *þing* sites. According to Sanmark, "In the early 20th century, two 'booth' sites in Greenland were identified, one at Brattahlíð (Qassiarsuk) and another at Garðar (Igaliku), which, after some debate, were accepted by leading scholars as the remains of thing (assembly) sites".[12] Russia was settled, and parts conquered, by Swedish peoples (the Rus) in the 800s, so the possibility of *þings* appears increasingly likely. Some scholars have argued that the Swedish Rus influenced early Slavic legal codes, so it is not far-fetched to imagine *þing* sites along the Volga.

Furthermore, while L'Anse aux Meadows shows evidence of Icelandic colonization circa 1000, there have been no traces of *þing* sites in the New

---

11 Owen, ed., *Things in the Viking World.*
12 Sanmark, "The Case of the Greenlandic Assembly Sites," 178.

World. However, I would not be surprised if evidence of a site was one day discovered. The *þings* appear to have been too much a part of the legal culture in medieval Scandinavia not to be used in the New World. As archaeologists continue their searches for Viking Age cultural centres, more *þing* sites will inevitably be discovered in the future.

The cultural power of the assemblies should not be overlooked. Classical scholars have argued for the performative aspects of manhood—since only males could publicly use rhetoric—and this is also true of medieval Nordic rhetoric. These *þings* were imbued by their users with rhetorical power. Those men allowed to speak at the assemblies were exhibiting power given to them by the assembled. The situatedness of the event—outdoors, surrounded by the community, weighing matters of law—created a rhetoric for legality. The medieval Nordic peoples valued this rhetorical space, and they took it with them wherever they colonized. But, more importantly, such legal power was a force to maintain public peace through redress of wrongdoings without having to resort to violence. While conflict did sometimes escalate to violence after court cases, the ultimate purpose was to diffuse this type of action through fines and other more civil forms of legal actions, including mediation and advocacy for parties concerned in the proceedings.

In Iceland, one of the greatest exemplars of this rhetorical space is derived from the Law Rock (*lögberg*). This natural, raised stone at the *þingvellir* commands a broad view of the plains surrounding the Óxara river. Moreover, since there is a basalt cliff behind it, the space has the effect of something like a natural amphitheatre, allowing the person holding the Law Rock to project his voice to the crowd. Thus, the Law Rock created both a rhetorical space to speak which was imbued with power and it was practically ideal for its ability to allow a speaker to wield that power. The amphitheatre acoustics along with the commanding presence upon the Law Rock create a significant element in the rhetorical performance between the speaker and the audience. Since there were blendings of legal matters and formulaic pieces, the crowd would potentially see the lawyer as they might view the performance of a skald, an Old Norse poet, so the speaker could command, captivate, and plead with his audience—an audience used to hearing a performance. When someone stepped to the Law Rock, the space in some ways defined the rhetorical situation. The spoken words needed to be legal, formulaic, performative, and clear.[13]

---

13 For a more in-depth discussion of literacy in medieval Scandinavia, see Lively, "In Search of Viking Literacy," 101–17.

The Viking Legal Tradition—The Icelandic Example

Viking society had a long tradition of judicial process. The Icelandic people developed a sense of democratic populism, almost unheard of in feudal continental Europe, very early in their history. While there were several cultural groups which settled Iceland,[14] the immigration of the Nordic peoples to Iceland slowed dramatically in the 930s. From this time until the reemergence of Norwegian royal influence in the 1200s, Icelandic culture operated mostly outside the sphere and influence of mainstream European culture. Such isolation led to the undisturbed development of legal institutions known only to Iceland. For instance, Iceland operated without influence from strong political or religious figures for almost 400 years, hearkening back to earlier times in Scandinavian customs. The sagas show us family life, with the major players in these stories always being located on the family farm holdings.[15] The harsh environment may have precluded the building of empire in Iceland. Consequently, this isolation and the difficult landscape led to many adaptations in the Norse culture to make it function.

The key adaptation I am looking at is the arrangement in Icelandic legal structure. The devolution of government into local community created a need to establish a legal system to deal with squabbles and disputes among the farm owners. The Icelandic term for these farm owners was *goðar* (sing. *goði*), which may have carried religious significance at one point.[16] Each *goði* controlled a holding as something of a chieftain, but he exerted little or no sway in military or political matters beyond his property lines. Each *goði* was supported by followers who were called *þingmenn* (sing. *þingmaðr*). The *þingmaðr* was a retainer who joined the household of a *goði* and attended the *þing* in his retinue. In turn, the *þingmaðr* promised to support and help his *goði* in legal actions. The *goði*'s relationship to his *þingmaðr* was not based in geography, as was typical in the feudal system emerging in continental Europe. For a chieftain in Europe, his power was derived from the geographical area he controlled, and his power was strengthened by the

---

14 Among the ethnic groups settling Iceland were not only Norwegians, but Irish slaves, a few Danes, and some relatives of original settlers from Viking Age colonies in the North Atlantic. For a broader discussion, see Ebensdóttir, "Ancient Genomes 1028–1032, and deCode Genetics, "The Majority of Icelandic Female Settlers."

15 For the purposes of this work, I draw mostly from the Family Sagas, which recount early stories of the settlement and the dealings of the Icelanders, the short tales, the *þáttr*, and the *Sturlunga sagas*, which trace the history of the Sturlung family.

16 See Jones, *History of the Vikings*, 282, where he describes the *goði* as a secular priest.

more area he held. In Iceland, the *þingmaðr-goði* relationship was more of a public commitment.[17] However, their relationship was tenuous at best. A *þingmaðr* was free to switch allegiance by simply swearing a public oath, and, as the sagas attest, *þingmaðr* all too often abandoned or betrayed a weak *goði*.

To settle disputes that inevitably arose, the Icelanders set up four regional assemblies, or *þings*, and, once a year, every summer, they met in one major assembly known as the *Althing* (*Alþing*). The chieftains would name judges to hear the cases and render rulings based in tradition and common sense, or reasonableness.[18] R. I. Page points out that the Icelanders were informed by common sense, which I argue is a form of *hóf*. Here, Page relates how Ari Thorgilsson explains how the Icelanders reasonable resolved communal conflicts at the *Althing*:

> There arose a great legal dispute at the *thing* between two people, Thord gellir, son of Olaf feilan from Breidafiord, and Odd, known as Tungu-Odd, who came from Borgarfiord. Odd's son Thorvald had taken part with Hoensa-Thorir in the burning of Thorkel Blundketil's son in Ornolfsdal. Thord gellir was the prosecutor in the case because Herstein, the son of Thorkel Blund-Ketilsson, was married to his niece Thorunn...The defendants were prosecuted at the *thing* held at the place which was later called Thingnes in Borgarfiord, because it was then the legal requirement that homicide cases should be pursued at the thing that was nearest the spot where the killing occurred. But the two sides fought there, and the *thing* could not be conducted according to law. There Thorolf 'fox', brother of Alf of the Dales, was killed; he was in Thord gellir's party.
>
> Later they brought the case before the *Althing*, and there the two sides fought again. In this broil men from Odd's party fell: moreover Hoensa-Thorir was outlawed and later killed, and others too who had taken part in the burning.
>
> Then Thord gellir made a speech about it at the Law-rock pointing out what problems men had if they must go to unfamiliar *things* to bring suits for homicide or injuries done them, and he spoke of what he had had to go through before he could bring his case to law and the various troubles that would arise if no solution could be reached.
>
> Then the land was divided into Quarters, so that there should be three *things* in each where members of the same *thing* could bring their lawsuits;

---

17 For a more in-depth discussion of the *goði-þingmaðr* relationship, see Byock, *Viking Age Iceland*, 118–41.

18 Ari Thorgilsson, the famous Icelandic historian (1067–1148 CE), gives examples of the Viking legal mind and the idea of reasonableness (*hóf*) in dealing with legal matters in the *The Book of the Icelanders*.

except that the Northern Quarter there should be four because the north-erners were not prepared to accept anything else.[19]

Þingadeild mikil varð á miðli þeira Þórðar gellis, sonar Óleifs feilans ýr Breiðafirði, ok Odds, þess es kallaðr vas Tungu-Oddr; hann vas borgfirzkr. Þorvaldr sonr hans vas at brennu Þorkels Blund-Ketilssonar með Hœsna-Þóri í Ǫrnolfsdali. En Þórðr gellir varð hǫfðingi at sǫkinni, af því at Hersteinn Þorkelssonr Blund-Ketilssonar átti Þórunni systurdóttur hans. Hon vas Helgu dóttir ok Gunnars, systir Jófríðar, es Þorsteinn átti Egilssonr. En þeir váru sóttir

á þingi því es vas í Borgarfirði í þeim stað, es síðan es kallat Þingnes. Þat váru þá lǫg, at vígsakar skyldi sœkja á því þingi, es næst vas vettvangi. En þeir bǫrðusk þar, ok mátti þingit eigi heyjask at lǫgum. Þar fell Þórolfr refr, bróðir Álfs í Dǫlum, ýr liði Þórðar gellis.

En síðan fóru sakarnar til alþingis, ok bǫrðusk þeir þar þá enn. Þá fellu menn ýr liði Odds, enda varð sekr hann Hœsna-Þórir ok drepinn síðan ok fleiri þeir [es] at brennunni váru.

Þá talði Þórðr gellir tǫlu umb at lǫgbergi, hvé illa mǫnnum gegndi at fara í ókunn

þing at sœkja of víg eða harma sína, ok talði, hvat hónum varð fyrir, áðr hann mætti því máli til laga koma, ok kvað ýmissa vandræði mǫndu verða, ef eigi réðisk bœtr á.

Þá vas landinu skipt í fjórðunga, svá at þrjú urðu þing í hverjum fjórðungi, ok skyldu þingunautar eiga hvar saksóknir saman, nema í Norðlendingafjórðungi váru fjǫgur, af því at þeir urðu eigi á annat sáttir.[20]

Consensus-building and appeasement seemed to be a rhetorical stance here because the concessions received in the other quarters was not acceptable to the Northern Quarter. So, the acceptance of the unusual fourth court in the north was a reasonable, common-sense approach to securing the legal system needed to keep the peace.

An Icelandic lawyer was called a lawman (*lögmaðr*), and the main official was given the prestigious title of Lawspeaker (*lögsögumaðr*). Even though these various courts were for public consumption—dealing with criminal, civil, and judicial matters—the men who could hear and speak well in the law gained some prestige among their peers. For cross-jurisdictional cases that could not be settled in the *þings*, the Vikings set up the Fifth Court at the *Alþing*—a sort of appeals court to the four regional things.

Since the legal proceedings were a cultural event, the judicial process became an important social construct in Iceland, and legal rhetoric became

---

19 Qtd. in Page, *Chronicles of the Vikings*, 176.

20 *Íslendingabók* in AM 113 b fol.

a valued skill among the people. As time went on, the society became dominated by legalistic principles that judged almost every facet of life. A *goði*
might be called upon to know the law regarding tariffs, divorce, sheep stealing, kinslaying, and outlawry. Because of the diverse nature of the legal institution, those talented in law became a prized commodity, not only as lawyers but also as advisors to their *goði*. A lawyer (*lögmaðr*) needed an excel-
lent memory and a quick recall to plead cases effectively in court.

At the *Alþing*, the collected *goðar* elected a Lawspeaker (*lögsögumaðr*)
for a term of three years. The Lawspeaker was commissioned with reciting
one third of the collected law each year of his term. As one can imagine, this
recitation was haphazard at best. Since the Lawspeaker was not necessarily
elected because of his memory or eloquence, they often only recited the law
they could remember. If the Lawspeaker was of lesser quality, then the recitation was undoubtedly flawed. Thus, the law was fluid in early Iceland. The
Lawspeaker would stand on a rocky outcropping, the Law Rock (*lögberg*),
to recite the law, accompanied by several others who would help correct
him. The Law Rock also served as the place where litigants made their com-
plaints public. When a suit was brought forth, the *goðar* appointed forty-
eight judges to hear the case. The number and distribution of judges were
based on the four regional *þings* and occasionally varied in numbers. Many
of the *goðar* served as judges, but trusted *þingmenn* were elected as well.

When presenting a case, Icelanders preferred to settle disputes with
a sensible monetary payment—ironic considering the modern reputation
Vikings have for violence. In a culture where personal honour was highly
valued and respected, sometimes an offer of restitution could be considered
insulting if it were deemed insufficient to satisfy honour. Therefore, violence
sometimes occurred in court cases. *Njal's Saga* opens with a scene of such
violence: Mord Fiddle's case opens with an attempt to settle a dispute mon-
etarily and ends with a duel, foreshadowing the latter case in the saga as
Njal's killers are put on trial.[21]

The title for this chapter, "Loud Approval at the Law Rock," is taken from
Njal's Saga.[22] This refers to the successful completion of a case with the audience's approval, since the audience was essential to the praise and shame
culture and needed to observe and make sure the legal proceedings were
within the bounds of social propriety. The legal process was considered
almost sacrosanct among the Icelanders. A verbal approval by the gallery
listening to the case meant that the verdict would be viewed as binding by

---

21 See *Njal's Saga*, trans. by Magnusson and Palsson, 290–323.

22 *Njal's Saga*, trans. Magnusson and Palsson, 298.

the communities. Since Iceland had no police force or constabulary, winning public approval meant that this judgment would be upheld by the people—a very democratic way to enforce judgments. This tradition of popular approval is a very old Germanic tradition. Tacitus comments on the noisy approval in Germania. "If a proposal displeases them, they shout their dissent. If they approve, they clash their spears. Showing approval with weapons is the most honourable way to express assent."[23]

Bringing weapons to court was a time-honoured tradition among the Germanic peoples. In *Njal's Saga*, Bjarni Brodd-Helgason tells Flosi Thordarson, "Also, we must always go fully-armed to court and be continually on our guard, but never fight unless we are forced to do so in self-defence."[24] While this might appear humorous to modern readers, to a Viking audience this was a serious piece of advice. Violence between parties was a legal option of the time. If the parties could not agree on mediated settlement or if a side sought revenge, then violence was a way to end the matter. Dueling (or *hólmganga* in Old Norse) was an armed meeting between sides, and it was an acceptable appeal for a case that could not litigiously reach a conclusion. However, duelling was often frowned upon by the public because if parties were injured or killed, the conflict might lead to wider public strife.

However, if a person were murdered, killed in a duel, or died unexpectedly, the bounds of law were still considered to be enforceable even after death. If ghosts appeared, Vikings could hold a door-court, or a *duradómr*, to rid the house of the dead. In *Eyrbyggja's Saga*, for instance, Thoroddr and his men, who had drowned, haunted the farmhouse of Kjartan, causing sickness, death, and all range of ill omen for those in the farmstead. The door-court was held like a *þing*, and charges of trespassing against the ghosts resulted in their banishment. The following example from *Eyrbyggja's Saga* illustrates the power of the legal mindset in medieval Scandinavia:

> It was Candlemas Eve when they came to Frodriver, and the fire had just been lit. Thurid had been taken ill with the same illness as those who had died. Kjartan went straight into the living room and saw Thorodd and the other dead people sitting at the fire as usual. He pulled down the canopy from Thorgunna's bed, plucked a brand from the fire, went out, and burnt to ashes all the bed furnishings that had once belonged to Thorgunna.
>
> Next Kjartan summonsed Thorir Wood-Leg, and Thord the Cat summonsed Thorodd for trespassing on the home and robbing people of life and health. All the dead were summonsed in the same way. Then the door-court was held and charges made, the proper procedure of ordinary law courts

---

23 Tacitus, *Agricola and Germania*, 43.

24 *Njal's Saga*, trans. Magnusson and Palsson, 291.

being observed throughout. The jury was appointed, testimony was taken, and the cases were summed up and referred to judgement. When sentence was being passed on Thorir Wood-Leg, he rose to his feet and said, "I've sat here as long as people would let me." Then he went out through the door at which the court was not being held.

After that, sentence was passed on the shepherd, and he stood up. "I'll go now, and it seems I should have gone sooner," he said.

When Thorgrima Witch-Face heard her sentence, she stood up, too. "I've stayed here as long as you've let me," she said.

So they all received their sentences one after another; and each, on being sentenced, got up, made some such remark, and left the room. It was clear that none of them wanted to go.

Thorodd was the last to be sentenced. When he heard the judgement, he stood up. "There's no peace here," he said, "we'd best all be on our way." And with that he walked out.[25]

Síðan riðu þeir út til Fróðar ok kvǫddu menn af næstum bœjum með sér um leið ok kómu til Fróðar um kveldit fyrir kyndilmessu í þann tíma, er máleldar váru gǫrvir. Þá hafði Þuríðr húsfreyja tekit sótt með þeim hætti, sem þeir er látizk hǫfðu. Kjartan gekk inn þegar ok sá, at þeir Þóroddr sátu við eld, sem þeir váru vanir. Kjartan tók ofan ársalinn Þórgunnu, gekk síðan í eldaskála, tók glóð af eldi ok gekk út með; var þá brenndr allr rekkjubúnaðrinn, er Þórgunna hafði átt.

Eptir þat stefndi Kjartan Þóri viðlegg, en Þórðr kausi Þóroddi bónda, um þat, at þeir gengi þar um hýbýli ólofat ok firrði menn bæði lífi ok heilsu; ǫllum var þeim stefnt, er við eldinn sátu. Síðan var nefndr duradómr ok sagðar fram sakar ok farit at ǫllum málum sem á þingadómum; váru þar kviðir bornir, reifð mál ok dœmð; en síðan er dómsorði var á lokit um Þóri viðlegg, stóð hann upp ok mælti: "Setit er nú, meðan sætt er." Eptir þat gekk hann út þær dyrr, sem dómrinn var eigi fyrir settr.

Þá var lokit dómsorði á sauðamann; en er hann heyrði þat, stóð hann upp ok mælti: "Fara skal nú, ok hygg ek, at þó væri fyrr sœmra."

En er Þorgríma galdrakinn heyrði, at dómsorði var á hana lokit, stóð hon upp ok mælti: "Verit er nú, meðan vært er."

Síðan var sóttr hverr at ǫðrum, ok stóð svá hverr upp, sem dómr fell á, ok mæltu allir nǫkkut, er út gengu, ok fannsk þat á hvers orðum, at nauðigr losnaði.

Sídan var sókn felld á Þórodd bónda; ok er hann heyrði þat, stóð hann upp ok mælti: "Fátt hygg ek hér friða, enda flýjum nú allir." Gekk hann þá út eptir þat.[26]

---

25 *Eyrbyggja Saga*, trans. Pálsson and Edwards, 140–41.

26 *Eyrbyggja Saga*, Íslenzk Fornrit, 151–52.

Even in death, the drowned Icelanders had to obey the law. This passage shows the legal mindset and the rhetorical power of the court. Ghosts were banished by witnesses who testified as proof of the ghosts' trespassing. There is no Christian religious exorcism here—no pleas to God to cleanse the farm. The law was binding in the minds of the Icelanders. The priest only arrives after the ghosts have fled. The power of legal words, spoken in open court beneath the sky, had the real power here, and even the dead had to acknowledge that power.

The Forensic Rhetorical Education

The Viking world was organized around a legalistic mindset that valued technicalities of law. William Ian Miller contends, "The saga genre itself attests to the cultural obsession with law."[27] In Icelandic society, being a *lögmaðr*, or lawman, was a valued commodity. However, education in the Viking world was neither standardized nor institutional. In fact, historians generally omit Nordic education in the scope of their scholarship. However, we can look at the evidence given to us in commentaries and the sagas to better understand the education undertaken by a *lögmaðr* in medieval Scandinavia.

The medieval Norse were isolated as a culture, yet their educational system was fairly consistent with the rest of Europe in the early Middle Ages. The Icelanders, for instance, had few established church schools in Iceland until the 1200s. However, scholars can glean a sense of the educational methods by examining historical accounts and sagas. As was typical of the rest of Europe, apprenticeships and fosterage were the typical methods for allowing young, male, Icelandic students to gain an education. While this is not necessarily supported by the preponderance of evidence in the sagas, there are a few passing references to show that rhetorical education took place by apprenticeship or fosterage with men who were regarded as having keen legal minds. For instance, in *Njal's Saga*, we see Njal offer to become a "foster-father" and teacher of the law to Thorhall Ásgrimsson as part of a wedding agreement:

> After the wedding, Njal offered to become foster-father to Thorhall Asgrimsson, and Thorhall went with him to live at Bergthorsknoll. He lived there for a long time, and came to love Njal more than his own father. Njal taught him law so well that he later became the greatest lawyer in Iceland.[28]

---

27 For further discussion, see Miller, *Bloodtaking and Peacemaking*, 227.

28 *Njal's Saga*, trans. Magnusson and Pálsson, 85.

En eptir veizluna bauð Njáll Þórhalli Ásgrímssyni til fóstrs, ok fór hann til hans ok var með honum lengi síðan. Hann unni meira Njáli en fǫður sínum. Njáll kenndi honum lǫg, svá at hann varð mestr lǫgmaðr á Íslandi.[29]

There are a few other passages in the sagas that show a clear social institution of apprenticeship for legal training. The next example is taken from *Gunnlaugs saga ormstungu*, or *The Saga of Gunnlaugur Snake's Tongue*. Gunnlaugur is in training to be a skald. When he becomes angry with his father, he leaves to apprentice with Thorsteinn, a *lögmaðr*, to learn the law.

> Then Gunnlaug rode off and arrived down at Borg that evening. Farmer Thorsteinn invited him to stay and he accepted. Gunnlaug told Thorsteinn what had happened between him and his father. Thorstein said he could stay as long as he liked, and he was there for a year. He studied law with Thorstein and everyone thought well of him.[30]

> Gunnlaugr reið þá í brott þaðan ok kom um kveldit ofan til Borgar, ok bauð Þorsteinn bóndi honum þar at vera, ok þat þiggr hann. Gunnlaugr segir Þorsteini, hversu farit hafði með þeim feðgum. Þorsteinn bað hann þar vera þeim stundum, sem hann vildi, ok þar var hann þau missari ok nam lögspeki at Þorsteini, ok virðist öllum mönnum þar vel til hans.[31]

And, similarly, in *The Droplaugarssons*, there is an additional clue to the case of fosterage. Unsatisfied with the settlement at the spring *þing* in his district, Helgi Droplaugarsson seeks an apprenticeship with Thorkel to learn the law.

> The next Spring Thorkel Geitisson, Grim and Helgi went to the Krakaloek Spring Assembly in Fljotsdale. There they met Helgi Asbarnarson and settled the suit for the killing of Thorgrim with money paid by Thorkel. But Helgi Droplaugarsson did not like it that money should be paid for Dungbeetle's killing and he considered the slander to be unavenged. The brothers stayed on in Krossavik and Helgi learned the law from Thorkel. Helgi was involved in a great many lawsuits, especially in those against the thingmenn of Helgi Asbarnarson.[32]

> Um vá rit eftir fóru þeir Þorkell Geitis son ok Grímr ok Helgi til Forsdals til Korkalǫkjarvárþings. Þar hittusk þeir Helgi Ásbjarnar son ok sættusk á víg Þorgríms, ok lauk Þorkell fé fyrir. En Helga Droplaugar syni glíkaði illa. er fé kom fyrir víg Torðyfils, ok þótti óhefnt illmælisins. Þeir brǿðr váru í Kros-

---

29 *Brennu-Njáls Saga*, Íslenzk Fornrit, 74.

30 "The Saga of Gunnlaug Serpent-Tongue," trans. Attwood, 566.

31 *Gunnlaugs saga ormstungu*, The Icelandic Saga Database.

32 *The Fljotsdale Saga*, trans. Hawthorne and Young, 81.

savík, ok nam Helgi lǫg af Þorkatli. Helgi fór mjǫk með saksóknir ok tók mjǫk sakir á þingmenn Helga Ásbjarnar sonar.[33]

It is interesting to note that in the oral-tradition age of Iceland, when *lög-menn* were acknowledged for their unique talents with the law, the court proceedings were conducted in the common tongue—or the low style, as it is known to scholars. In contrast, the skalds used an intricate style, common in oral cultures, which displayed poetic virtuosity and was not easily mimicked by the population. The skaldic verse was considered the high style. The oral poetry was entertainment but not everyone could engage in it, while the law seemed to be for widespread public consumption.

The populist roots of the law pleadings and court cases were accessible to anyone who was attending the *þing*. This is quite a bit different to modern court cases where the judicial language relies on knowing a highly technical jargon of legal terms derived in large part from the Greek and Roman jurist tradition. In modern society, participating in the law is not for people without the proper training. Few people without legal training can easily understand the vocabulary, much less the nuances of language in our modern courts. In Iceland, the law was made for public consumption and the average man's participation at the *þings*.

While the idea of legal training and accessibility runs counter to our modern conceptions of law, there are even a few short passages in the sagas that show people playing at court. In the *Ljótsvetninga Saga*, Thorkell Geitisson is credited with creating "the rules of the mock court"[34] where bondsmen and servants would get together and convene courts for the entertainment of the chieftain and his retainers. In *Njal's Saga*, peasant children "chattering loudly with the folly of youth"[35] hold a mock court where they make fun of a chieftain's infidelity.

The rhetorical education among the Icelanders followed a different course than the Greco-Roman tradition. Unlike the Greek and Roman training, there are no records of something akin to a collected Icelandic *progymnasmata*.[36] The only things that come close are the *Poetic Edda* and the *Skáldskaparmál* found in Snorri's *Prose Edda* which offer lists of tropes, fig-

---

33 AM 132 fol. (141va.3–147vb.4) – *Droplaugasona saga.*

34 Andersson and Miller, *Law and Literature*, 150.

35 *Njal's Saga*, trans. Magnusson and Pálsson, 55.

36 *Progymnasmata* were rhetorical exercises used throughout the Greek and Roman worlds to train students in the use of rhetorical device. Perhaps the two most famous works of *progymnasmata* are the works of Aphthonius the Greek and his teacher Libanius.

ures, and kennings for skalds to draw upon rather than rhetorical exercises to practice.

Shown in brief passages, legal games of the mock courts appear to have been a way that commoners could learn law. Much like any other endeavour in the Middle Ages, apprenticeship and fosterage were ways in which skills were passed from one generation to another. However, Iceland's populist slant gave the legal rhetoric to the people. From the highest chieftain to the lowest freeman, the people needed to have, at the very least, a rudimentary understanding of law and legal procedure—a very reasonable thing to do.

Rhetoric in Viking Legal Proceedings

To the reader familiar with the history of rhetoric, a lot of the usual rhetorical devices are missing from the medieval Nordic repertoire. When Aristotle discusses the types of forensic rhetoric, he mentions the need for *pisteis*, or techniques of persuasion. In contrast, the Icelandic court did not use persuasion, as we think of it. The sagas and *The Grágás* show us very formulaic methods for prosecuting and defending a case. The lawyers recited formulaic pieces followed by witnesses who had to recite formulaic pieces. If anyone misspoke, then the other side could easily claim an irregularity in court and ask for a dismissal. This focus on the formula makes sense because Icelandic society privileged oral formulas. In *Njal's Saga*, as Mord Valgardsson began the prosecution of Flosi Thodarson at the Law Rock, he recites the form in a very precise manner:

> Mord named witnesses—"to testify that I give notice of an action against Flosi Thordarson for the unlawful assault, inasmuch as he assaulted Helgi Njalsson at the place where he assaulted and inflicted on him an internal wound, brain wound, or marrow wound, which did cause Helgi's death. I demand that Flosi be sentenced to full outlawry on this charge, not to be fed nor forwarded nor helped nor harboured. I claim that all his possessions be forfeit, half to me and half to those men in the Quarter who have a lawful right to receive his confiscated goods. I refer this manslaughter action to the proper Quarter Court. I give notice of action to be heard at this session, for full outlawry against Flosi Thordarson, as assigned to me by Thorgeir Thorisson."[37]

> Mǫrðr nefndi sér vátta:—"nefni ek í þat vætti," segir hann, "at ek lýsi lǫgmætu frumhlaupi á hǫnd Flosa Þórðarsyni, er hann hljóp til Helga Njálssonar á þeim vættvangi, er Flosi Þórðarson hljóp til Helga Njálssonar ok veitti honum holundar sár eða heilundar eða mergundar, þat er at ben gerðisk, en

---

37 *Njal's Saga*, trans. Magnusson and Pálsson, 298.

Helgi fekk bana af. Tel ek hann eiga at verða um sǫk þá sekjan skógarmann, óalanda, óferjanda, óráðanda ǫllum bjargráðum; tel ek sekt fé hans allt, hálft mér, en hálft fjórðumgsmǫnnum þeim, er sektarfé eigu at taka eptir hann at lǫgum. Lýsi ek vígsǫk þessi til fjórðungsdóms þess, er sǫkin á í at koma at lǫgum; lýsi ek lǫglýsing; lýsi ek í heyranda hljóði at lǫgbergi; lýsi ek nú til sóknar í sumar ok til sektar fullrar á hǫnd Flosa Þórðarsyni. Lýsi ek handsel-dri sǫk Þorgeirs Þórissonar."[38]

This passage shows the Viking legalistic mind at work. Mord fails to incite the crowd and condemn Flosi in the manner for which Aristotle would advo-cate in *On Rhetoric*.[39] Since Mord does not need to invent the wording of the charges, his speech would be deemed *atechnic*[40] by the Greeks, which was a lesser form of oratory that required less skill on the speaker's part. When the Vikings developed their law, their sense of "for the common good" rested on a publicly constructed set of values. The Vikings had other ideas about the common good because of their praise and shame culture as well as their strong honour culture. Based on earlier Scandinavian law practices, the Icelandic courts did not necessarily move with the idea of the just and the unjust. For this reason, the Viking court did not attempt to attack the character or motives of the defendant. Rather, it was simply asserted that someone had taken an action and deprived someone of life or property, and it needed to be redressed. Actions by the defendants were usually acknowl-edged publicly, so the courts could see the action to be mollified legally. If not, a feud would erupt, and the consequences might be severe for the over-all community.

While this thinking may seem different to the Greeks, the Romans under-stood the need for law to be a mediating force. Cicero, for example, in his *De Oratore and De Inventione*[41] recognizes that lawful use of the courts can have a positive effect in keeping the peace. However, Cicero's ornate style and use of amplification and stasis are foreign ideas to a Viking court. Even later in Viking history, when the church established Iceland as a Christian nation and the Vikings had access to classical learning, the canonical texts of rheto-ric did not take hold immediately. Rather, it would take almost two hundred years before Christian culture, including educational practices, would come to dominate the land.

---

38 *Brennu-Njáls Saga*, Íslenzk Fornrit, 374–75.

39 For further details, see Aristotle, *On Rhetoric*, trans. Kennedy.

40 Aristotle, *On Rhetoric*, 37.

41 Cicero's *De Oratore* and *De Inventione* mention rhetoric's possible use for public peace.

The bridge from orality in the proceedings to a written culture was some time in the making. Early on, the Vikings used the Younger *Futhark*, the runic alphabet, but laws generally were not written in this alphabet.[42] The inscriptions in the Younger *Futhark* were epitaphs, runic poems, rune sticks, and runestones. The vernacular Old Norse writing occurred after the introduction of Christianity in Iceland and, in particular, after the general conversion of Iceland was achieved—at least symbolically and in typical legalistic fashion—by the judgment of the *Alþing* that Iceland would be a Christian nation.

The newly introduced Latin literacy in Iceland led Norse churchmen to begin writing the sagas and laws of Iceland into the vernacular, not Latin, so once again it could belong to the people. Perhaps the most famous Icelandic Historian was Ari Thorgilsson. He wrote the earliest surviving history of Iceland, the *Íslendingabók*. Ari's book traced the earliest settlements of Iceland in the vernacular language. The precedent for using the vernacular led to the creation of a written law code.

Together, the *Konungsbók* and the *Staðarhólsbók*[43] collected the existent laws into a codified whole, known as the *Grágás*, or "Grey Goose" laws. (Scholars are uncertain why these collected laws are known as the *Grágás*, but there is some speculation.)[44] Once these laws were written, the law books could be referenced by litigants, and the professionalization of the lawyers had begun.

Women in the Viking Legal World

The rhetorical stance of medieval Nordic women seems almost a contradictory idea. On one hand, the society is structured as a highly masculinized and male-dominated, with women being excluded from even speaking in court. On the other hand, no other society in Europe at the time gave women the amount of cultural importance as medieval Scandinavia. Women could inherit property, run farms, and divorce their husbands if they chose. It is a

---

42 The Futhark is a runic alphabet. Scholars believe that these runes may have migrated north from the Romans; however, Richard Leo Enos suggests that they may have come from the earlier Etruscan alphabet.

43 For a comprehensive examination of the *Grágás*, see *Laws of Early Iceland: Grágás I*, trans. Dennis, Foote, and Perkins, and *Laws of Early Iceland: Grágás II*, trans. Dennis and Foote.

44 There is quite a bit of speculation of the origins of the term "Grey Goose" laws (*Grágás*). Some believe that it must have gotten its name from the goose quill used to compose them. While still others believe that the term is an idiom whose meaning is now lost to us.

mixed bag of cultural suppression and liberation which makes the rhetoric developed by the medieval Nordic women so fascinating. There is also the geography to consider. Since many of the Scandinavian settlements were isolated, the women needed to contribute in significant ways. The lifestyle was mostly subsistence, and the women and men needed to be equal in many ways because the work of survival and defence needed to be done. The demands of geographical space account for a lot of the equality represented in the sagas.

In *Rhetoric Retold*, Cheryl Glenn frames the argument for women's rhetoric in the classical tradition:

> Rhetoric always inscribes the relation of language and power at a particular moment (including who may speak, who may listen or who will agree to listen, and what may be said); therefore, canonical rhetorical history has represented the experience of males, powerful males, with no provision or allowance for females. In short rhetorical history has replicated the power politics of gender, with men in the highest cultural role and social rank. And our view of rhetoric has remained one of a gendered landscape, with no female rhetoricians (theoreticians) clearly in sight.[45]

Her argument is compelling when looking at the classical and Christian traditions, but the saga world complicates this in some ways. Yes, the legal roles were limited to men in the courts, but *The Grágás* laws explicitly state the legal rights for women. As women grew older, they were granted more and more power to run their lives. This seems like splitting hairs, since the laws were codified by men, but an average medieval Scandinavian woman probably had many more legal and social rights than her sisters in Christianized Europe.

The sagas show the rhetorical practices women engaged in as forms of civic rhetoric. Women had a great deal of influence in the function of society. The sagas portray many strong women characters who are not silenced. The reasonableness of the situation gave them a means to interact civilly in ways that many women in Christianized Europe were not permitted. They spoke in longhouses, travelled extensively, and managed and inherited wealth. The *Laxdæla Saga*, for instance, paints a realistic picture of women's roles in medieval Iceland. It is also one of the few sagas with major female characters. Guðrún and Hallgerðr occupy a majority of the text and show that women are not satisfied with being controlled by men and restricted to live on a farm. There are many examples in the sagas where women exercise control and use the rhetoric at their disposal to influence the course of events.

---

45 Glenn, *Rhetoric Retold*, 1–2.

Arbitration and Mediation in Legal Actions

In order to prevent wider contention, there were mechanisms in place to help stop legal disputes from escalating further. Essential to such preventative mechanisms, Norse advocates and mediators were generally known as *góðviljamaðr* (pl. *góðviljamenn*), literally "a good-will man," or *góðgjarnmaðr* (pl. *góðgjarnirmenn*), meaning "benevolent men." The terms show how these advocates and mediators were viewed publicly as men who helped keep the peace, and they were seen as reasonable and worthy of positive linguistic terms. These men of good will would insert themselves, or be asked to insert themselves, into a dispute to help broker some type of peace before the situation escalated to either a court case brought to the *Alþing* or, worse, to violence.

The men who worked as advocates and arbitrators were generally regarded as honourable men. In the societal framework of praise and shame, these men were seen as keepers of the peace and defenders of the social fabric, and this would increase their reputations as reasonable men, bringing greater social prestige to their families. Regardless of how their efforts eventually turned out, the sagas provide a positive portrayal of their attempts to broker peaceful settlements. Women were banned from taking part in official legal proceedings, but, according to the sagas, they were often involved in mediation and violence abatement.

Beyond the societal restraints on an arbitration to reduce violence, the society demonstrates an impressive ability to wield rhetorical power in order to limit violence. In the intricate web of relationships among *goðar*, they found that they could further cement their power in a region by working as arbitrators. Considering the need for an arbitrator to appear reasonable, the use of this skill in legal disputes meant that the concerned parties in a conflict would then owe the arbitrators some kind of favour, further strengthening the ties among people in the region. The arbitrators, therefore, undertook these duties with some self-interest in mind, as they aimed to further solidify their positions in the region. Additionally, they realized that conflict and open hostilities were not good for anyone, and it could permanently harm their districts if not curtailed.

As Byock sees it, "In many ways arbitration was a face-saving procedure. It relied upon the understanding that the honor of all parties was to be considered, and it allowed the parties to withdraw from a critically dangerous situation."[46] With the reputation of both parties on the line, the rhetorical savvy of the arbitrators had to be keen. They had to look for ways to inter-

---

46 Byock, *Feud in the Icelandic Saga*, 103.

pret the situation or spin the facts, so that all parties were able to leave with their honour intact and no possible slights occurred to the injured parties. The problem with arbitration is that it relied on the goodwill of the parties entering into such negotiations as well as the goodwill of the arbitrators. If one party was unreasonable, then negotiations would be difficult to establish or maintain.

Conclusion

The legal mindset of the medieval Scandinavians formed an overarching structure to police unruly behaviour and mitigate potentially violent situations. The creation and success of *þings* across the Viking Diaspora showed the importance of these courts and legislative bodies to the Norse. When Vikings settled somewhere, their legal structures went with them. The negative view that these people were "lawless" couldn't be further from the truth, because the rhetorical power of the *þing* site was potent to the Norse people.

The sagas describe in detail how these legal and legislative *þings* were conducted. We have several court descriptions in the sagas, and we have several law codes from the medieval period across Scandinavia. These court dealings inform us about the successes and challenges of the social order from the time, and they show how a clear rhetorical stance of *hóf*, or reasonableness, motivated much of the dealings at these assemblies. The medieval Scandinavians would rather build consensus than engage in pitched battle with their countrymen. *Hóf* dictated a way to move forward with very contentious litigation or legislative problems without threatening the stability of the communities involved.

Good men who entered the legal profession or acted as mediators to help preserve the peace are described in very positive terms. The lawyer is admired at least as much as a heroic warrior. Reasonable men who knew the law were held up as cultural icons. Lawyers were trained in legal pleadings, and the courts were geared towards more arbitration and mediation to preserve the peace and avoid a descent into violence. The commitment to reasonableness in community dealings strengthened relationships and the societal fabric that was needed in a society which lacked a strong central government. *Hóf*, as a rhetorical stance in civic and legal affairs, brought a level of stability to the Viking Diaspora throughout the medieval period.

Chapter 7

LEGAL REASONABLENESS IN ACTION

FOUR CASE STUDIES

> "If we tear apart the law, we tear apart the peace"
>
> *Íslendingabók*[1]

EXAMPLES OF LEGAL rhetoric are common in the family sagas, which deal with broader issues surrounding forensic rhetoric and the rhetorical stance of *hóf* that influences it. The family sagas trace more explicitly how this cultural and rhetorical practice of reasonableness manifests itself in actual legal proceedings.[2] For this purpose, an examination of court cases in *Njal's Saga*, *Ljósvetninga Saga*, *Bandamanna Saga*, and the Case of the Conversion of Iceland are used as *foci* to better illustrate how *hóf* influences the legal setting. By closely examining these representative cases, it allows us a glimpse into the mindset of the participants and offers further evidence that reasonableness is the first preferred value in the legal dealings of the Scandinavians.

Njal's Saga

The story of Njal's burning is a tragic story of blood feud. What starts as an insult by Njal's wife becomes a bloody tale which culminates in a group of men, led by Flosi Thordarson, burning Njal's longhouse down and killing him along with his family and retainers. Only one person, Kari Solmundarson—Njal's son-in-law—escapes in the smoke of the fire to join friends and bring a case against the burners at the *Alþing*. In my opinion, no court case in the sagas better illustrates forensic rhetoric than does this one. The case deals

---

* Small portions of this chapter previously appeared in Lively, "We Must Always Go Fully Armed," 81–96.

1 Thorgilsson, *The Book of the Icelanders*, 9.

2 Aristotle describes the concept of *phronesis*, a similar idea of reasonableness like *hóf*, in *Nicomachean Ethics*, where he contends that reasonable listeners on the jury will be swayed by the facts of the case, and their good character. The Roman jurist tradition used the term *prudentia*, which stressed the reasonable, normal social mores should be upheld by the populace and, thus, by the jurors in a case.

with the claim brought against Flosi[3] and the men who trapped Njal, his wife, and their retainers in his hall and burned them all alive. At the *Alþing*, the case is brought to bear, and the ramifications are witnessed by both the participants and the readers alike.

According to Jesse Byock, feuds in sagas can be resolved in three ways: "(1) arbitrated settlement, whether in or out of court; (2) direct settlement between parties, whether violent or peaceful; (3) the rejection of an offer of resolution."[4] The case of the burning of Njal encompasses these three elements of feud, thus showing the deft use of legal rhetoric in *Njal's Saga*. The importance of reasonableness should not be undervalued here. Two of the three means of resolution are peaceful. This means that violence was the last resort of a failed arbitration, and it was often averted completely. The case of Njal's burning is well detailed, allowing us glimpses at the legal proceedings in Iceland. The saga details how reasonable people tried to adjudicate a measured settlement after the tragedy in order to ensure violence did not disrupt the community. Thus, the legal benefits of reasonableness kept the settlements peaceful and, at least, nominally cooperative to ensure stability of society.

For this case, the saga specifically sets up the major lawyers and their credibility—Mord and Thorhall, the prosecutors, and Eyjolf the defence lawyer. Mord and Eyjolf are portrayed as two of the best lawyers in Iceland.[5] Here are some examples taken from *Njal's saga* that demonstrate legal expertise:

> There was a man called Mord Fiddle, who was the son of Sighvat the Red. Mord was a powerful chieftain, and lived at Voll in the Rangriver Plains. He was also a very experienced lawyer—so skillful, indeed, that no judgement was held to be valid unless he had taken part in it.[6]

> Mǫrðr hét maðr, er kallaðr var gígja; hann var sonr Sighvats ins rauða. Hann bjó á Velli á Rangárvǫllum. Hann var ríkr hǫfðingi ok málafylgjumaðr mikill ok svá mikill lǫgmaðr, at engir þóttu lǫgligir dómar dœmðir, nema hann væri við.[7]

---

3 Flosi reluctantly takes up the feud against Njal, but once he does, he is utterly ruthless, leading up to the climactic burning of Njal.

4 Byock, *Feud in the Icelandic Saga*, 259.

5 In the sagas, those who were especially adept lawyers were often cited and praised by the saga authors.

6 *Njal's Saga*, trans. Magnusson and Pálsson, 39.

7 *Brennu-Njáls Saga*, Íslenzk Fornrit, 5.

LEGAL REASONABLENESS IN ACTION | **99**

Later, the reader is introduced to Eyjolf, another prominent lawyer in the saga:

> A man called Eyjolf Bolverksson was one of the three greatest lawyers in Iceland. He was a man who commanded great respect, and his knowledge of law was outstanding. He was extremely handsome, tall, and strong, with all the makings of a fine chieftain. He was also very fond of money, like the rest of his kinsmen.[8]

> Eyjólfr hét maðr; hann var Bǫlverksson...Eyjólfr var virðingamaðr mikill ok allra manna lǫgkœnastr, svá at hann var inn þriði mestr lǫgmaðr á Íslandi. Hann var allra manna fríðastr sýnum, mikill ok sterkr ok it bezta hǫf-ðingjaefni; hann var fégjarn sem aðrir frændr hans.[9]

Thorhall's participation is important because he has been trained in law by Njal himself—the greatest lawyer in Iceland before his murder. The case in *Njal's Saga* seems very contemporary in many ways. Our predisposition to legality and litigiousness seems right at home in the medieval *Alþing*, and the legal manoeuvrings of Eyjolf, Mord, and Thorhall seem worthy of any television legal drama.

When each of the parties arrives at the *Alþing*, they are seeking support. In the Icelandic legal system, it is common for the litigants to bring their supporters with them to court. This show of force creates an immediate, sympathetic audience, and it seems to have had the effect of creating a situation wherein the court of public opinion works in conjunction with societal values to create, or reinforce, a legal right.

At the *Alþing*, Kari solicits the help of Mord and other relatives and allies of Njal to help bring the case. Allied with them is Thorhall, a man whom Njal provided training in the law. When they go to the Law Rock to bring the case against Flosi and the burners, they bring witnesses to swear formulaic oaths before the judges at the court. An example from the text shows the formulaic nature of the words: "that I give notice of an action against Flosi Thordarson, inasmuch as he inflicted on Helgi Njalsson an internal wound, brain wound, or marrow wound, which did cause Helgi's death, at the place where Flosi had previously made an unlawful assault on Helgi."[10] Over the course of the proceedings he uses this formulaic piece several times. The *Alþing* had a large number of judges: forty-eight were available to hear the case, but the plaintiff and defendant could exclude six each, so judgments were usually done by thirty–six judges. The Law-Speaker served as more of a legal scholar and parliamentarian to the proceedings. The point here is not

---

8 *Njal's Saga*, trans. Magnusson and Pálsson, 290.

9 *Brennu-Njáls Saga*, Íslenzk Fornrit, 363.

10 *Njal's Saga*, trans. Magnusson and Pálsson, 298–99.

one where facts need to be ascertained. The men admit it, and the witnesses swear to it. In the Norse world, it would be considered cowardly to deny an action committed in the public sphere. While this does occur in several sagas, hiding a crime like this would be considered socially unacceptable and legally dubious.

To defend against the case brought against him, Flosi approached Eyjolf Bolverksson who was considered the third best lawyer in Iceland. At the onset, he refuses to take up Flosi's case due to the nature of his crimes, but Flosi bribes him with a very valuable gold armband—even though it is illegal in Icelandic law to bribe a lawyer. Flosi's rash action of burning the house, his denial of the under-siege access outside (to meet in fair fighting), and his need to bribe a lawyer show the seriousness with which Flosi, and the readers, should view the case against him.

Both Flosi and Mord visit the booths of the various chieftains, each seeking support for their cases. Flosi is asked by his lawyer, Eyjolf, to seek an arbitrated settlement, but Flosi refuses. Eyjolf attempts a reasonable course to keep the peace, but it is rejected by his client, so Eyjolf must try other tactics to win the case. The first possible peaceful solution to the feud is rejected.

Because of the severe nature of the crimes against Njal, his family, and their retainers, Mord asks the court for full outlawry as a verdict, which meant that Flosi and the men accused would have to leave Iceland forever. This is a much harsher charge than lesser outlawry, which required only a three-year exile. This sets the stage for the court case. Since Flosi rejected the arbitrated settlement, the risk is high: either win or leave his home and holdings forever.

Mord pleads well at the Law Rock and the judges seem to favour him, but Eyjolf finds clever ways to diffuse Mord's case. First, he has Flosi transfer his chieftaincy to his brother, so Mord will appear to have prosecuted in the wrong court. Then, he sets out to challenge the jurymen. This sets up a repetitive theme of Mord pleading, Eyjolf countering the charges, and Mord having to seek help from Thorhall. Thorhall, however, cannot go to the Law Rock because he has a boil on his leg the day of the trial. One of the themes that come from this sequence in the trial is that law is meant to keep the peace in society, while legal manoeuvrings like those displayed by Eyjolf threaten to destroy the civil peace. In each instance, frustration builds in the prosecuting lawyers, and the witnesses must continually appear in court to speak their formulaic testimony before the judges. As Thorhall comments to Mord, "Tell them that they should not let themselves be tricked by lawyers' quibbles."[11] Since Eyjolf knows his case in defence of Flosi is weak, he tries to undermine

---

11 *Njal's Saga*, trans. Magnusson and Pálsson, 305.

the jurisdiction and process of the case itself. Eyjolf isn't worrying about the facts, nature, or seriousness of the issue. He concedes these as lost, instead he attacks the legal process itself.

As the case progresses, Eyjolf tries to undermine the proceedings by challenging the swearing in of the jury, saying that their relation to the pleader disqualifies them. However, Thorhall observes the legal standing of the *Alþing* by contending that the only legal reason for denying a sitting juror is a relationship to the plaintiff rather than the lawyer. This begins a game of one-upmanship between the lawyers. Eyjolf tries to invalidate the jurisdiction again by claiming that dependent householders couldn't sit as jurors, but Thorhall once again explains that the householders can serve if they "own milch animals."[12] Eyjolf then tries to get jurors excluded because they live too far from the scene of the crime, but Thorhall precisely states the law that only a majority of jurors needed to be living near the crime scene. With further legal trickery by the defence, the narrator notes that the gallery, who had been observing this back and forth, saw that Flosi and Eyjolf were trying to undermine the proceedings. The sagas states, "There was loud agreement…that Flosi and his men were resorting to mere lawyers' quibbles and cheating."[13] This observation is true, as Flosi and Eyjolf find a loophole and win the case. Eyjolf, seeing that his case was about to fail, claimed that the whole proceeding was invalid because the jurisdiction was incorrect—it had been pleaded in the wrong quarter court.

At this point, Thorhall lances his wound and comes forward claiming direct settlement through violence. He loved Njal as a father, and having Flosi go free is unacceptable to him. He rejects the idea of resolution, and, enraged at the devious undermining of the judicial proceedings, grabs a spear and attacks the supporters of the burners. A general battle ensues, and as the two sides engage in combat Flosi is wounded and Eyjolf is killed—as are many of their supporters.

It is ultimately Hall of Siða—whose son, Ljot, died fighting for Flosi—who ends the case by asking for a settlement on equal terms. He pleads for a settlement to stop the killing. He asks for no compensation for his loss, and he asks only that the case against Flosi be heard and judgment passed. In the end, Flosi is sentenced to full outlawry and ordered to leave Iceland. Several of Flosi's men are sentenced to three years' outlawry. Several others are fined for fighting, but Eyjolf is given no compensation because he was an unfair and dishonest lawyer. The men at the *Alþing* are so impressed by

---

12 *Njal's Saga*, trans. Magnusson and Pálsson, 306.
13 *Njal's Saga*, trans. Magnusson and Pálsson, 307.

Hall of Siða's plea for peace that they pool their money to compensate him anyway.

> It remains to be said that after Hall of Siða had forgone any compensation for his son in order to bring about a settlement, everyone at the Althing contributed something to compensate him. It amounted to no less than eight hundred ounces of silver—a quadruple compensation. But all the others who had been on Flosi's side received no compensation for injury, and were extremely dissatisfied about it.[14]

> Nú er þar til máls at taka, er Siðu-Hallr er, at hann hafði lagit ógildan son sinn ok vann þat til sátta, þá bœtti honum allr ðingheimrinn ok varð þat eigi minna fé en átta hundruð silfrs, en þat váru fern manngjǫld. En allir aðrir, þeir er með Flosa hǫfðu verit, fengu engar bœtr fyrir vansa sinn ok unðu við it versta.[15]

As demonstrated by Eyjolf's legal manoeuvring, the idea of jurisdiction was fundamental to the way the Vikings perceived their legal system. The gallery observing the case seems to get more and more frustrated with Eyjolf and Flosi because they are misusing a respected legal institution. The audience at the court respected the law and the jurisprudence associated with keeping the peace. On a regular basis, the normal operations were for the courts to help with settlements and keep the peace. Examining *hóf* in terms of the traditions in medieval Scandinavia allows scholars to consider questions relating to how the medieval Norse legal mind may have thought about the issues involved in legal disputes and how the society found ways to prosecute wrongdoers while simultaneously keeping the peace in places that had no formal constabulary to enforce the judgements of the courts. *Njal's Saga* presents an unusual case of feud that circumvents the legal system and leads to pitched battle. Most often, though, a successful case led to "loud approval at the Law Rock."[16]

Njal's Saga may be read as a cautionary tale that illustrates that reasonableness is the best course of action during a feud. The saga's tragedy occurs because the principal actors in the case often start at reasonable means but slowly become unreasonable. The saga ends with a return to reasonableness, as Hall of Siða calls for an end to hostilities and no compensation for his family. The observers see this as an ultimately selfless and reasonable event. He is practicing *hóf* in the public sphere, and the bystanders are so impressed with his actions that they pool their own money and compensate him for his loss.

---

14 *Njal's Saga*, trans. Magnusson and Pálsson, 323.

15 *Brennu-Njáls Saga*, Íslenzk Fornrit, 414.

16 *Njal's Saga*, trans. Magnusson and Pálsson, 298.

Ljósvetninga Saga

The *Ljósvetninga Saga* illustrates the many uses of arbitration, as men of goodwill attempt to stifle the violence and unreasonableness of the saga's antagonists. The saga is quite episodic, composed of a series of connected tales, or *Þáttr*, which connect to the main saga.[17] The major contention is between the brothers, Solmund, Eyjolf, and Soxolf—who are described as "all forceful and overbearing men"[18]—and Ofeig Jarngerdarson—who is portrayed as a powerful but relatively moderate man. Ofeig embodies the Nordic ideal of a reasonable man. He acts in the best interest of the population to keep the peace and make sure the Ljósvatn area doesn't erupt into violence. The major episodes in the saga create clear delineations between moderate and immoderate conduct. The reasonable courses of action are the acts of those who seek arbitrated and moderated settlements.

Chapters six and seven are called *Ofeig's þáttr* (a *þáttr* being a short tale). This section of the saga sets up the major conflict between the people of Modruvellir and the Ljóvetnings, which runs throughout the rest of the saga. This narrative is led by Ofeig, and the saga is a comparison of Ofeig's attempt to keep the peace while Gudmund is portrayed as unreasonable in dealing with his neighbours. Gudmund would often travel with a large retinue and stay with his *þingmenn* for long periods, basically pauperizing them. When the *þingmenn* appeal to Ofeig, complaining about Gudmund's behaviour, he decides to show Gudmund the error of his ways. So, Ofeig brings a large retinue and stays with Gudmund for a long time, draining the resources of the *goði*. Gudmund sees the problem caused by his travels and changes his habits. When Gudmund comes to Ofeig's house, Ofeig gifts him with a pair of ruddy coloured oxen. Gudmund gives a gift of black oxen in return. The saga comments that "Ofeig's reputation had grown greatly because of these dealings with Gudmund."[19] Ofeig's reputation as a man of goodwill, as evidenced by this *þáttr*, is important to later dealings of arbitration in the saga.

Another instance of mediation occurs in *Vǫðu-Brands Þáttr*, when Harek's rude and insulting behaviour brings him into conflict with Vodu-Brand. Vodu-Brand ends up slaying Harek, who is described in the saga as "a great champion: he did not pay compensation for the men he killed."[20]

---

17 These *þáttr* are *Sǫrla Þáttr*, *Ófeigs Þáttr*, and *Vǫðu-Brands Þáttr*. Anderson and Miller's translation includes the *þáttr* inserted in the *Ljósvetninga Saga* itself for a more complete narrative.

18 Andersson and Miller, *Law and Literature*, 122.

19 Andersson and Miller, *Law and Literature*, 144.

20 Andersson and Miller, *Law and Literature*, 147.

Harek's unwillingness to pay compensation breaks social protocol of redressing a harm against a family. When the two fight, Harek is killed by Vodu-Brand with an axe stroke to the head. Two brothers step in and agree to mediate, and Vodu-Brand agrees to pay the family compensation for the killing. Since Harek was ill-tempered, the family agrees to the compensation; thus, all parties save face. Having been insulted by Harek before their fight, Vodu-Brand saves his reputation by standing up to Harek; the mediating brothers gain reputations as moderate men; and Harek's family gains the compensation they deserve in a public setting. These elements of rhetorical mediation appear throughout the saga, enforcing the theme of *hóf* both to the characters in the sagas and to the readers.

However, Vodu-Brand's character is not moderate by nature. Rather, throughout the saga, he is reminded by others to be moderate. After the killing of Harek, Vodu-Brand lives with his father, Thorkel Geitisson. Vodu-Brand is moody, drinks too much, and refuses to converse with his father, who reminds him, "You are a very erratic fellow. Now return to your sociable ways in moderation".[21] Brand ignores his father's advice, and he injures one of Gudmund's retainers during a sporting match. Thorkel tries to arrange compensation, but Gudmund flatly refuses, wanting to take the injury to court. Thorkel doesn't have the funds or resources to properly defend his son in court, so he rides to the *þing* with only five retainers. Thorkel is hoping to find an arbitrator to seek a mediated settlement.

When Gudmund brings the case to court, Thorkel stands and offers Gudmund a self-judgment (*sjálf-dœmi*). This public display of contrition by Vodu-Brand's father acknowledges wrongdoing on the part of his son and allows Gudmund to name his compensation. This gesture should have moved Gudmund to accept the settlement. The eyes of the court were now turned to Gudmund to do the right thing: to accept Thorkel's proposal and agree to a reasonable settlement of gold, silver, or livestock. Rather than act reasonably, Gudmund stubbornness causes him to refuse. Thorkel again asks,

> "We are still willing to guarantee a settlement for the man if you will accept a self-judgment," Thorkel said.
>
> Gudmund said that he wasn't inclined to prosecute the man in their district if they had a mind to void the case: "the man is definitely going to be outlawed."[22]

---

21 Andersson and Miller, *Law and Literature*, 151.

22 Andersson and Miller, *Law and Literature*, 156.

Þá mælti Þorkell Geitisson: "Þat vilda ek, Guðmundr, at þú tœkir sættir ok
sjálfdœmi, sekðalaust."

Guðmundr svarar: "Þat mynda ek þiggja, ef þú ættir eptir duganda mann
at bjóða. En nú nenni ek eigi um vanmennu þá, er ek hefi svá starfa fyrir
haft."[23]

The two sides then prepare for battle, but Ofeig and Thorstein—both moderate men—try to avert the bloodshed: "Thorstein said, 'since you are
friendly with both parties...We should take a chance with his brother, Einar.
It would be more advisable to seek a settlement.'"[24] This focus on mediation
for a settlement is the quintessential moment of *hóf*. The public has seen
the events unfold at the *þing*, and they realize that a peaceful settlement can
save face for all parties involved and help maintain civic peace. When they
seek out Einar, Gudmund's brother, he further strengthens the idea of moderation. "We are friendly with both parties and have an obligation to work
for reconciliation."[25]

This theme of moderate thinking and resolve is carried throughout
the rest of the saga. Gudmund's stubborn character and power constantly
threaten to derail the rhetorical practices. While it seems as if the power
structures are more potent than peaceful settlements, the resolve of the
social fabric endures. Einar marries Thorkel's daughter, and he acts as a
mediator between the two families because he is now tied to both houses.

When Gudmund has a feud with another person and brings a court case,
the saga says, "Efforts were made to bring about a settlement, but Gudmund said it was pointless."[26] Later, Gudmund claimed that a man named
Thorir had stolen livestock. Gudmund brings him to court, but Thorir again
claims, "You [Gudmund] know no moderation in your aggressiveness."[27] This
dispute lasts some time until violence once again seems inevitable. At the
Alþing, Thorir and Gudmund are at the point of open warfare, but the saga
author once again states, "efforts were made to reach a settlement."[28] Thorir
goes to the Law Rock to challenge Gudmund to combat. However, before violence ensues, Thorir calls for mediation one last time:

---

23 *Vǫðu-Brands Þáttr*, Íslenzk Fornrit, 134.

24 Andersson and Miller, *Law and Literature*, 157.

25 Andersson and Miller, *Law and Literature*, 157.

26 Andersson and Miller, *Law and Literature*, 174.

27 Andersson and Miller, *Law and Literature*, 178.

28 Andersson and Miller, *Law and Literature*, 181.

"Many of our friends and distinguished men have put themselves out to mediate our case, said Thorir. "They reproach me for not wanting to offer money for the offenses with which you charge me. I shall now put an end to this. I propose to make the offer just that much better to make up for the long delay: I will accept your brother Einar's binding arbitration."

"I will accept no arbitrator in this case but myself," declared Gudmund.[29]

Þá mælti Þórir: "Vinir várir margir ok gǫfgir menn hafa lagt sik til þess at ganga í milli um málaferli okkur, ok veita þeir mér ámæli fyrir þat, at ek vilda eigi fé bjóða fyrir sakar þær, er þú hefir á hendr mér. Skal nú eigi svá lengr fram fara.: Vil ek nú bjóða þér því betr sem ek hefi lengr frestat: Þat eru handsǫl mín ok gǫrð Einars bróður þíns."

Guðmundr svarar: "Engum manni ann ek at gera um þessi mál nema sjálfum mér."[30]

Gudmund's declaration leads to Thorir's exile, but it does not stop Gudmund's behaviour. The feuds started by Gudmund last into his sons' generation. Only then are they able to establish a settlement that brings an end to Gudmund's uneven behaviour.

Ljósvetninga Saga acts as a warning to the readers that they need to be respectful of the law, be reasonable, and be moderate. Gudmund's actions show what misuse of power can be and lead to if unmoderated. The Ljósvetnings have a moderate temperament, and throughout the saga they show a respect for the law. While the power balance clearly falls with Gudmund and his kin, the ultimate victory belongs to those who practice *hóf*.

Bandamanna Saga

Bandamanna Saga is a short saga centred around the rise of Odd Ofeigsson and the schemes of several powerful *goði* who attempt to steal his lands and wealth. The protagonist of the saga is Odd, the son of Ofeig, descendant of the Ofeig Jarngerdarson in *Ljosvetninga Saga*. While Ofeig is a wise and well-respected man, he has little money or disposable wealth. His son, Odd, feels this gives them very little status, so he asks his father for an inheritance. Odd leaves the farm and takes fishing equipment with him. He then spends three years as a fisherman, earning money until he can buy goods and become a trader. He invests in a ferry and a trading business which earn him a lot of money. After several years of this, he invests in a long-range trading ship and goes abroad, where he becomes increasingly wealthy.

---

29 Andersson and Miller, *Law and Literature*, 182.

30 *Ljósvetninga Saga*, Íslenzk Fornrit, 39.

Eventually, he returns to Iceland, but he has no title or lands and, therefore, is not a *goði*. Odd finds land and establishes a successful farm in Northern Iceland, at Mel. He becomes a *goði*, and his kinsman Vali manages his farm and advises him on important matters. Among other workers, Odd hires a man named Ospak, who is strong but has a rather bad reputation. Ospak becomes a valued member of the farm, but Odd becomes bored with farming and wants to travel again. Vali wants to travel with Odd, so Odd transfers the *goðorð* to Ospak for the time they are gone and leaves him in charge of the farm.

Odd and Vali return two winters later, wealthy from their travels, but Ospak holds back on returning the farm and *goðorð* to Odd. Finally, Odd threatens Ospak with an axe, and Ospak returns the ownership of the farm. However, Odd's sheep start disappearing, and Ospak is suspected. Vali rides to Ospak's farm to see about the sheep and tries to broker a peace with between them: "I'll ride up to the house and meet with Ospak and see if he is willing to come to terms".[31] Vali is acting as an arbitrator to help settle the dispute because he knows both parties. He is attempting to diffuse the situation, but he is ambushed and murdered by Ospak. For the murder of his kinsman, Odd takes Ospak to court.

At court, Odd tries prosecuting the case himself, but he is not trained in law as his father was. So, even though he had more money and lands, his father had more legal knowledge. Odd makes a legal mistake, and the case is thrown out on a technicality. Ofeig witnesses the problem and offers to help his son. He approaches the jurors and asks, "Did there seem to you any kind of justice in paying attention to such a triviality instead of condemning a thoroughly bad man, a thief, and a murderer?"[32] He uses logic on them, knowing that they swore oaths to uphold the law, and he argues the law is "an oath to judge as fairly as you know how."[33] He offers them silver as compensation to avoid "breaking your sworn word,"[34] persuading them that they could be rid of a truly bad man.

Following Ofeig's intervention, Ospak is outlawed for killing Vali. The men gathered believe that Odd has pursued the case with "determination,"[35] and they look to Ofeig as the legal mind behind this victory. Several powerful men conspire to pursue Ofeig's action as a bribe to the jurors, and they

---

31 "Saga of the Confederates," trans. Ellison, 472.
32 "Saga of the Confederates," trans. Ellison, 475.
33 "Saga of the Confederates," trans. Ellison, 476.
34 "Saga of the Confederates," trans. Ellison, 476.
35 "Saga of the Confederates," trans. Ellison, 477.

try and outlaw Odd (rather than Ofeig) and gain self-judgment against him. Ofeig tells his son to give him a portion of his possessions and to take the rest of his wealth and load it aboard his ships, so the conspirators can't take his wealth if they win the case, thus making it a hollow victory.

Ofeig then takes up the defence of his son and uses the idea of reasonableness against the conspiring confederates. Ofeig goes to the Law Rock and talks directly to the people: "I have stayed out of the case against my son Odd up to now, even though it was begun in such a scandalous fashion that no one can think of a parallel."[36] When he calls the first witness of the eight opponents of Odd, he asks him how mediation works, questioning whether these agreements are between two men over a wrong or if they are among eight men against one. The crowd sees that the chieftains are entering into an unlawful prosecution of eight against one. This clearly breaks the civic function of mitigating a claim that could break out into violence. Eight against one looks like a conspiracy to gain Odd's wealth rather than a lawful action, and the chieftains will lose face, reputation, and honour if they continue with the case against Odd. Ofeig effectively nullifies their plan by changing the case to look at their motives, making it risky for them to prosecute. When Ofeig reveals all that is left of Odd's wealth is thirteen ounces of silver, and he has taken the rest out of Iceland, one of the conspirators says, "everyone can see that this settlement is pointless and silly."[37] Another told Ofeig, "Well might you pat yourself on the back! No one man can ever have taken the wind out of the sails of so many chieftains" (492).

Ofeig's counsel makes the confederates' demands seem silly and unreasonable, and he uses this to put their status and honour into question. The potential shame of the court case, held in front of the people of their districts, directs the confederates back toward a more moderate path. Ultimately, Ofeig's plan was to show the confederates their immoderate behaviour and bring them back into the fold of respectable, reasonable citizens.

The Conversion of Iceland

In the late 900s, Christianity was on the march across northern Europe. Denmark had nominally converted in 826, and Norway officially converted circa 995. Although there had been Christians in Iceland even early in its history, the old gods and the new one seemed to coexist peacefully until the missionaries began arriving. After the conversion of Norway, Norwegian

---

36 "Saga of the Confederates," trans. Ellison, 487.

37 "Saga of the Confederates," trans. Ellison, 491.

king Olaf Tryggvason (r. 995–1000) began a campaign to Christianize Iceland. Rather than helping his cause, the early missionaries he sent were disrespectful to the traditional culture and often violent in their missionary activities.

The conversion of Iceland offers a glimpse into *hóf* in a recorded historical case. There are several sources which recount the Icelandic conversion to Christianity. *Njal's Saga* contains an account of the conversion and dates it to the year 1000, but the most convincing source is Ari Þorgilsson´s account in the *Íslendingabók*, which was written a mere sixty-seven years after the conversion. Ari interviewed living witnesses when composing his historical treatise. In support of Ari's account, Byock traces Ari's family history as well as his educational history:

> He [Ari] was brought up at Haukadalr by Hall Thorarinsson, who lived to the age of ninety-four and who remembered being baptized as a child of three by the missionary Thangbrand. Ari was also the student of Teit Isleifsson. Teit was the son of Iceland's first bishop, Isleif, who was the son of Gizur the White, a participant in the events of the conversion.[38]

Ari's attempt to use first-hand accounts helps develop a clear sense of the events of the time.

The adoption of Christianity started with more conflict than conversion. The *Landnamabók* mentions a few settlers being Christian in the early days, but it seems that they got along well enough with their neighbours until missionaries arrived and began a campaign to convert the Icelanders. Even before Olaf Tryggvason's missionaries were dispatched after 995, Thorvald Konradsson the Far-Traveller's early attempt ended with two pagans dead and the start of the conflict between pagans and Christians.

This minor conflict remained simmering, but relations between the pagans and Christian Icelanders were not openly hostile until Olaf Tryggvason became the King of Norway. Upon his ascent to the throne, he began a systematic effort to convert the pagans in the North Atlantic. At first, Olaf sent Stefnir Thorgilsson, who seemed more criminal than Christian, destroying public images and pagan temples. Since this went against established law, Stefnir ran afoul of the public sentiment in Iceland. Ferguson notes that "it is some indication of their alarm at Christianity's intolerant nature that, in a direct response to Stefnir's activities, Icelanders now turned to the law to discourage the fanaticism of the followers of that religion."[39] Pagan and Christian Icelanders had been living in peaceful coexistence for over a hun-

---

38 Byock, *Viking Age Iceland*, 298.

39 Ferguson, *The Vikings*, 300.

dred years at this point. However, the "muscular brand of Christianity"[40] represented by Stefnir and Olaf caused the Icelandic people to view the new type of Christianity as unreasonable. Stefnir's actions were viewed as *óhóf*— a clear and unreasonable attacks against the beliefs of people who had not wronged him. This called for legal action. Eventually, Stefnir was outlawed. His public display of unreasonableness by publicly harming others' property showed him to be *ójafn*, and he needed to be removed from the civic body. At the *Alþing*, he was branded an outlaw, and families were asked to prosecute Christians in their ranks, which was a form of kin-shaming (*frændaskömm*). This historical and rhetorical act which was intended to make a reasonable law to stop the tension and violence occurring with the missionary failed horribly. This move intended to keep the peace only inflamed the Christian King of Norway, and Olaf was not deterred. He sent another missionary named Thangbrand, who had been successful in converting in Norway and the Faroe Islands. Thangbrand did convert a few prominent Icelandic *goði*, but he killed several people who wouldn't convert, and he was forced out of the country and back to Norway and Olaf's court.

Angry that his multiple attempts to convert the Icelanders had failed, Olaf Tryggvason responded by placing an embargo on Iceland. He wouldn't allow trading between Icelandic merchants and continental Europe. Since Norway was Iceland's main trading partner, this threatened to cripple the already fragile Icelandic economy. Faced with increasing animosity among Christians and pagans, and with a threat of economic and military action from Norway, Iceland seemed primed for massive social upheaval.

At the *Alþing* the following year, things came to a head. Christians and pagans skirmished and threatened to plunge the court and legislative process into chaos. Charges were brought against both sides. Thorgeir Thorkelsson was elected the Lawspeaker for the court to hear the case. Thorgeir was accepted by both sides since he was both a pagan and friendly with Christians, including several in his extended family.

So, instead of following through with further violence and conversion by the sword, the Icelanders followed their primary rhetorical stance and acted with *hóf* to try and find a peaceful settlement to the dilemma. Both sides pleaded their cases before the court. Afterwards, Thorgeir went into seclusion for a few days as he weighed his decision. On one hand, he needed to honour the gods of his forefathers and the history of his people. On the other hand, he needed to appease the Norwegian king to avoid invasion and make sure the Christians would lift the embargo. When he returned to the court,

---

40 Ferguson, *The Vikings*, 300.

he summoned both sides and made them swear publicly that they would abide by his decision. The *Kristni Saga* reports that when Thorgeir appeared he spoke the following:

> And I think it reasonable not to allow those to decide who are most contentious, and offer as compromise therefore among them that each side has points in its favor, but we all must have one law and a single faith, because as it will be agreed: if we dissolve the law, we break the peace.[41]

Another version is related in the *Íslendingabók*, as Ari writes of Thorgeir's decision.

> Then it was made law that all people should become Christian and those who here in the land were yet unbaptized should be baptized; but as concerns the exposure of infants, the old laws should stand, as should those pertaining to the eating of horseflesh. If they wished, people might sacrifice to the old gods in private, but it would be lesser outlawry if this practice were verified by witnesses.[42]

> Þá vas þat mælt í lǫgum, at allir men skyldi kristnir vesa ok skírn taka, þeir es áðr váru óskírðir á landi hér; en of barnaútburð skyldu standa en fornu lǫg ok of hrossakjǫtsát. Skyldu menn blóta á laun, ef vildu, en varða fjǫrbaugsgarð, ef váttum of kvæmi við. En síðarr fám vetrum vas sú heiðni af numin sem ǫnnur.[43]

From these examples it may be understood that Thorgeir was trying to develop a response that all parties would find equitable. He was relying on a position of reasonableness and an expectation that each side would uphold their oaths and abide by the decision. Furthermore, he was attempting to provide compromise by allowing people the worship of the old gods in the privacy of their own homes while having a clear façade of Christianity in the public sphere.

Anders Winroth suggests that, to the medieval churchmen, conversion should be more pronounced immediately. "The Christian convert must 'put off the old self' (Ephesians 4:22), including the Norse open pantheon of gods and any ritual or custom deemed pagan, and 'put on the new self' (4:24)".[44] Still, Byock suggests that the conversion took place in slower implements: "Christianity, coming peacefully to Iceland in 999 or 1000 (CE), did not

---

41 Qtd. in Gíslason, "Acceptance of Christianity," 242.

42 Qtd in Byock, *Viking Age Iceland*, 300.

43 *Íslendingabók* in AM 113 b fol.

44 Winroth, *Age of the Vikings*, 202.

uproot the established rural culture."[45] Based on the rhetoric of reasonableness and the civic fabric of Icelandic society, I favour the theory of a more
measured spread of Christianity, as many Icelanders would have needed
more time to adjust to the new religion. Proclaiming something to happen
and actually having it take place are usually two different things, which
Thorgeir seems to understand and account for in his decision.

When Thorgeir proclaimed Christianity as the religion of the land, he
doomed paganism in Iceland—although he probably did not realize it at the
time. He was attempting to make a reasonable solution to the conflict. Yet,
when we consider that this society was a shame culture, it becomes clear
that paganism couldn't survive. Considering the role of shame as a sort of
public policy, the accepted public form of religious consumption would be
Christianity. Even if a person worshipped the old gods in private, they would
have to adopt a public Christian persona. Facing such public scrutiny, and
with a person's honour and reputation in the balance, Christianity would
eventually force out pagan belief. This couldn't have happened quickly.
There would have been a slow attrition of pagans, as the public rhetoric of
Christianity became the religion of the land. In the *Íslendingabók*, Ari himself
suggests a slower, years-long timeline as well: "But a few years later this
heathen custom was abolished, as were the others."[46]

The four cases presented above relate to the seriousness with which the
medieval Scandinavians viewed *hóf* as a legal rhetorical position. With the
burden of potential violence erupting and destroying the civic fabric, these
arbitrators and lawspeakers needed to strike a balance between redressing
a legal wrong as outlined in their law codes and allowing the perpetrator
to save face with the community, where necessary. Unless the crime was so
egregious that it demanded full outlawry, the judgment had to be reasonable
enough to both acknowledge the problem and also prevent the harbouring
of ill-will between the parties involved, ensuring future peace.

The examples of *Njal's Saga* and the *Bandamanna Saga* show the importance of sound legal protections for people in legal disputes. These examples
demonstrate the problems which arise when men of power try to derail the
legal process for their own ends. If Flosi had accepted Njal's generous offer
of payment, then the hostilities could have been averted. Similarly, the chieftains who tried to illegally seize Odd's property in *Bandamanna Saga* tried
to unjustly use the law for nefarious purposes. What the reader should take
from these is that, according to Norse societal values, the law was supposed

---

45 Byock, *Feud in the Icelandic Saga*, 30.

46 Qtd in Byock, *Viking Age Iceland*, 300.

LEGAL REASONABLENESS IN ACTION | **113**

to be defended by men of good character and reasonableness who want to preserve the peace.

In the example in *Ljósvetninga Saga*, we see the problems that arise when an unreasonable man who won't compromise or abide by legal decisions, comes into power. His lack of regard for the law drags the district into conflict for a couple of generations. Only with the work of reasonable arbitrators is the conflict able to come to an end. Yet, Gudmund's example of *óhóf*, or unreasonableness, acts as a warning to the audience of the danger of such a stance. His rhetorical position of stubbornness endangered the entire district, disrupting civil society as well as the legal system over all of Iceland.

Finally, the historical example of the conversion shows the good will of the law in action. Thorgeir had legitimate and personal reason to side with the pagans, but he saw the bigger picture of society. He weighed the potential threat if he did choose his own beliefs. The public conversion to Christianity appeared to be a reasonable compromise between two competing systems, yet he didn't disenfranchise the pagan believers. He allowed them to continue to privately worship in the old ways. Both sides saved face, violence was averted, and the conversion, for the most part, was done peacefully in the traditional Icelandic way of law. Both sides exhibited goodwill with the judgment.

Conclusion: Towards A Nordic Legal Rhetoric

While trying to piece together a forensic rhetoric for the medieval Scandinavians, it has been necessary to build an inductive case. The evidence is scattered throughout the sagas and the histories, but some threads run through these works which allow some preliminary conclusions about the Vikings and their legalistic rhetoric.

First of all, the medieval Scandinavians held the letter of the law in high regard. The evidence of this is shown in their formulaic responses and their primacy of perfection of those formulae in the court pleadings. The Icelandic courts valued the precedents of the previous law, and the court depended on knowing the previously established law and what the public valued. The Norse valued a good memory, very much like in any culture who relied (at least in part) on orality. They did not seem to try to create a legal discourse outside of a prescribed set of phrases. Since the Vikings were a warrior culture, and likely depended on a mixed oral and functionally literate culture throughout the times the sagas take place, the idea of a man giving his word was important and binding—not only in oath-giving but in legal discourse as well. The medieval Scandinavians delighted in cunningly pleaded cases.

As such, the one-upmanship of the court proceedings in the sagas is often quite enjoyable for the reader, as lawyers find obscure points to best their rivals. However, the law gives certain parameters that should not be breached, as demonstrated by some of the examples presented here.

The medieval Nordic common idea of support in a legal dispute ultimately came down to might makes right. The first step in executing a case involved gathering warriors to support your case before the lawspeaker at the Law Rock. For the Norse lawyer, the *ethos* and *pathos* of the crowd were determined before they ever uttered a word in the case. The burden, and sometimes dilemma, of friendship and kinship are often more to the point of the cases shown in the sagas. However, these points may have resonated with the medieval readers of the sagas, because these dilemmas and the fragile thread of law versus violence were ever present in their local society. Yet, the courts and the arbitrators favoured reasonable settlements that saved face, avoided violence, and preserved honour in the public eye.

Conclusion

TOWARDS AN UNDERSTANDING OF NORDIC CIVIC AND LEGAL RHETORIC

"Wisdom is welcome, wherever it comes from."

Saga of the Confederates[1]

IN LATE SEPTEMBER of 1241, Snorri Sturluson—historian, priest, and the writer of the hugely important works the *Prose Edda* and the *Heimskringla*—was murdered in his home at Reykholt, Iceland, probably on the orders of King Haakon IV of Norway. Snorri had been an ardent defender of Icelandic culture. He was elected Lawspeaker at the *Alþing* twice, and he preserved the legends and mythology of the Nordic peoples in the *Prose Edda*. Snorri's importance to medieval Nordic culture cannot be overstated. Norway's machinations to annex Iceland accelerated after the assassination, and a little over a decade later, in 1252, Iceland would lose its independence, becoming a vassal to the Norwegian monarchy and effectively bringing the Viking age to a close.

By the 1250s, the vibrancy of the age was ending. The pagan north had been Christian for around 200 years, and the continental feudal system had mostly replaced the earlier chieftaincies of the Scandinavians. The expansion of the Viking Age was winding down, and the north was more fully enveloped into the culture of medieval Europe.

Considering the geography of the medieval north, most Scandinavians lived in rather rural, isolated farming and fishing communities, with the exception of a few large trading centres. The villagers had to cooperate in order to survive in the rough northern winters. They needed to be able to pool resources and work together on projects of food collecting and harvesting. Since these are village-oriented activities, the group needed cohesion to function effectively. For the safety of the community, the interactions of these people couldn't be severed with feud or violence. If they were, then everyone might perish in a harsh winter. So, the rhetorical stance of reasonableness was a common strategy among the villagers. Then, in the eleventh century, things changed. Scandinavian geography, which had long acted

---

1 "Saga of the Confederates," trans. Ellison, 491.

as a barrier from medieval European encroachment, eventually faltered as Norsemen in longships spread Christianity and feudal ideas into the north.

However, the cultural values of their civic and legal rhetoric remained strong. The *þings* still flourished across the north, and even with the imposed religious and governmental changes, the native traditions of the Scandinavians were resilient. Saga writers captured rhetorical elements of *hóf* in their writings, documenting the rhetorical tradition for posterity.

There seem to have been several independent factors at work which downplayed the rhetorical practices taking place in Scandinavia. The early Christian conflicts with the Vikings set the tone for the way they have been viewed over the past thousand years: violent, uncultured, and somehow lesser in the scope of Western European history. This is despite scholars like James J. Murphy attempting to break the stereotype of the "Dark Ages". Rejecting this isolation and diminishing of Scandinavian rhetorical culture, this examination of the Icelandic Sagas and the role of *hóf* in legal rhetorical and cultural practice allows us to expand our understanding of the era.

When looking at the context of the sagas, it is important to note that, as Byock explains, "Saga stories reveal the normative codes of the society and indicate to the reader basic rules of conduct."[2] Byock's research into the reliability of the sagas has informed the study of rhetoric presented here. Byock and other archaeologists have shown that many of the descriptions of events in the sagas are fairly reliable. Therefore, using literary references in the sagas can provide some insights into the rhetoric and frame of mind in the Saga Age.

Civic rhetoric has been defined in many ways. Aristotle defines his theory of rhetoric as being inseparable from civic engagement; thus, all rhetoric is civic in some way. Strecker and Tyler argue that culture and rhetoric are chiastic. So, where civic culture exists, there is rhetoric.[3] Grabill, on the other hand, defines Civic Rhetoric as "The theory and practice of civic involvement and citizenship."[4] In light of such observations, it is obvious that medieval Nordic culture had a robust civic rhetoric, for it had civic involvement in its town and legislative gatherings. However, the perception of civic rhetoric in the medieval period is often viewed as limited. For instance, Kennedy argues:

> even in the early Middle Ages, when there was reduced practical opportunity to exercise civic rhetoric, the definition and content of rhetorical theory

---

2 Byock, *Medieval Iceland*, 9.

3 See Strecker and Tyler, *Culture and Rhetoric.*

4 Grabill, *Writing Community Change*, 84.

set forth by Isadore and Alcuin, for example, show the same civic assumption: the revival of classical rhetoric in Renaissance Italy was foreshadowed by renewed need for civic rhetoric.[5]

Kennedy follows the typical view that rhetoric all but disappears in the medieval period, but his perspective of Scandinavia appears all too clear here. During the medieval period, Scandinavia had a clear and pressing need for civic rhetoric, and it had already developed a complex civic rhetorical culture. Its isolated geography and lack of feudal system gave the people a need to work as a civic unit, with democratic populism becoming the essential form of legislative control. The need for small communities to talk, make decisions, and regulate their small farmsteads, villages, and towns with words—rather than force—was much more common than the violent images often associated with the medieval north.

Though Roland Scheel questions the rhetorical aspects of law texts in Nordic society as "often decidedly 'anti-rhetorical,' or in any case highly specific rhetoric,"[6] the Family Saga corpus paints a highly rhetorical picture of civic and legal dealings steeped in rhetoric. The Norse civic and legal mindset was trained to reach a reasonable settlement involving a negotiated deal to keep the peace. The acknowledgement of this rhetorical presence in medieval Scandinavia is significant to understanding the civic and legal procedures of the time, which is still largely open to investigation. Sagas such as *Njal's Saga* and *Bandamanna Saga* illustrate the judicial complexities of the Viking Age, providing examples of the necessity of arbitration and reasonable settlements to avoid violence and ensure societal stability and cohesion.

To this end, the sagas suggest that the idea of reasonableness, or *hóf*, becomes essential to civic and judicial rhetorical moves. In a world where most people were armed in some fashion, keeping civic peace became one of the of the highest priorities. A person entering the public arena was supposed to be reasonable in all transactions and interactions they conducted. The ability to negotiate in this public sphere was considered a skill that kept the peace. Even with the power imbalances between *goði*, *bóndi*, and *þingmenn*, the need for a rhetoric of reasonableness to run the villages and *þings* is of utmost importance. Stability would have been important locally for the population, and a steady civic and legal landscape would have been of benefit to everyone, regardless of their social status.

---

5 Kennedy, *Classical Rhetoric*, 2–3.

6 Scheel, "Introduction."

I am not arguing that there was some kind of renaissance of medieval Scandinavian rhetors of the era, but there is a strong tradition shown in the saga corpus, with the examples discussed here revealing a complex historical framework set on *hóf* as the basis for public rhetorical acts. Violence was always there in the background, but it was ideally not the first recourse, nor was it expected to be. If a person was wronged, they were expected to seek a reasonable settlement first. A person could gain social prestige and improve their standing by seeking out settlements for themselves and helping others reach settlements as a mediator.

This village-sponsored rhetoric shaped public events and societal currents in the medieval north. Failing to recognize these currents of *hóf* in medieval rhetorical studies omits a great part of the core rhetorical principals practiced in medieval Iceland. The public roles in conflict resolution helped cement a public peace that was necessary in the isolated villages and towns that were so common across Scandinavia during the medieval period. This rhetoric spelled out roles in the public sphere, where such rhetorical techniques gave agency to the villagers in the determination of their civic lives. *Hóf* helped determine defined social roles, expectations, and faux pas. While some social stratification insulated *góði* from public scrutiny, the societal pressure was there to balance out unreasonable acts. Perhaps Else Roesdahl summed it up best:

> It is largely through the study of the Viking homelands, with their astonishingly high level of technical and organizational achievement, that our picture of the period has been altered...The Viking Age is now seen as having been altogether more complex, with a strong class system, diverse social conditions, and far more radical achievements"[7]

This complexity has often been overlooked in rhetorical studies. It seems that the early Christian chroniclers, who privileged Greco-Roman rhetoric, had a very effective anti-Northman propaganda campaign. The view of violent heathens is still a strong current in popular culture, and it is reflected in canonical rhetorical texts.

For decades, the "loss of rhetoric" narrative helped scholars view the Middle Ages as bereft of rhetorical activity. Bizzell and Herzberg's *The Rhetorical Tradition* claims that "During this thousand-year span, much Greco-Roman learning was lost...and Greco-Roman public forms of rhetoric all but disappeared." The great speeches and influence of rhetoric seemingly died with Cicero. But rhetoric did not disappear, "Christian scholars preserved

---

7 Roesdahl, *The Vikings*, 4–5.

and studied some of the surviving texts."[8] Bizzell and Herzberg set up the narrative that is generally accepted today, which is that Christians preserved Greco-Roman rhetoric to enlighten the heathen masses. However, Bizzell and Herzberg still fall into the reductive narrative of medieval Europe.

> For the next five centuries—sometimes termed 'The Dark Ages'—the sparse population of Europe survived in small local economic units...Even minimum subsistence could be swept away by marauding invaders—central Asians in the 400s, Arab Muslims in the 600s and 700s, and Asians, Muslims, and Norsemen in the 900s.[9]

It is obvious that in *The Rhetorical Tradition*, Bizzell and Herzberg are talking about the narrow focus of classical, Christian tradition. For some scholars, the Asians, Muslims, and Norsemen didn't have a place in rhetorical history, and their only purpose of such heathens was to destroy peoples who practised and used the proper kind of rhetoric. In the West, we were influenced to favour the classical, Latinate tradition. By looking at the Scandinavian population on the periphery of the Christian, classical West, we can reveal ways in which rhetoric was practiced in *different and productive* ways. It is important for scholars to shrug off these preconceptions of ignorance and violence which are often thrown onto medieval Scandinavia and, instead, we may examine the rich, complex rhetorical tradition that flourished there.

---

8 Bizzell and Herzberg, *The Rhetorical Tradition*, 431.

9 Bizzell and Herzberg, *The Rhetorical Tradition*, 434.

BIBLIOGRAPHY

Primary Sources

Adam of Bremen. *History of the Archbishops of Hamburg-Bremen*. New York: Columbia University Press, 2002.

AM 113 b fol. – *Íslendingabók* v. 1.0.4. Accessed July 7, 2023. https://clarino.uib.no/menota/text/menota/AM-113-b-fol.

AM 132 fol. (141va.3–147vb.4) – *Droplaugasona saga* according to AM 132 fol. (*Möðruvallabók*) v. 1.1, *Medieval Nordic Text Archive*, accessed July 6, 2023, https://clarino.uib.no/menota/text/menota/AM-132-fol-Droplaugarsona-saga.

AM 132 fol. (120vb.21–129rb.7) – *Kormáks saga* according to AM 132 fol. (*Möðruvallabók*) v. 1.1, *Medieval Nordic Text Archive*. Accessed July 1, 2023. https://clarino.uib.no/menota/catalogue.

Aristotle. *Nicomachean Ethics*, Translated by Terence Irwin. Indianapolis: Hackett, 1985.

———. *On Rhetoric: A Theory of Civic Discourse*. Translated by George Kennedy. Oxford: Oxford University Press, 1991.

Beowulf. Translated by Seamus Heaney. New York: Norton, 2000.

The Book of Settlements. Translated by Herman Pálsson and Paul Edwards. Winnipeg: University of Manitoba Press, 1972.

Brennu-Njáls Saga. Íslenzk Fornrit 12. Reykjavík: Hið Íslenzka Fornitafélag, 1954.

"Egil's Saga." In *The Saga of the Icelanders*. Edited by Jane Smiley. Translated by Bernard Scudder. New York: Penguin, 2000.

Egils saga Skalla-Grímssonar. The Icelandic Saga Database. Maintained and edited by Sveinbjorn Thordarson. Accessed June 6, 2023. https://sagadb.org.

Eyrbyggja Saga. Translated by Hermann Pálsson and Paul Edwards. New York: Penguin, 1989.

Eyrbyggja Saga. Íslenzk Fornrit 4. Reykjavík: Hið Íslenzka Fornitafélag, 1935.

Fadlan, Ibn. *Ibn Fadlan and the Land of Darkness: Arab Travellers in the Far North*. London: Penguin, 2012.

Faereyinga Saga. Translated by Volundr Lars Agnarsson and F. York Powell. Scotts Valley: CreateSpace Independent, 2012.

The Fljotsdale Saga and The Droplaugarsons. Translated by Eleanor Haworth and Jean Young. London: Dent, 1990.

Gísla Saga Súrssonar. Íslenzk Fornrit 6. Reykjavík: Hið Íslenzka Fornitafélag, 1943.

Gisli Sursson's Saga and The Saga of the People of Eyri. Translated by Martin Regal and Judy Quinn. London: Penguin, 2004.

Gunnlaugs saga ormstungu. The Icelandic Saga Database. Maintained and edited by Sveinbjorn Thordarson. Accessed June 6, 2023. https://sagadb.org/.

Hávamál. Edited by David A.H. Evans. vol. 3. London: Viking Society for Northern Research, 1986.

Heiðarvíga Saga. Accessed July 6, 2023. www.snerpa.is/net/isl/heidarv.htm.

Hrafnkel's Saga and Other Stories. Translated by Hermann Pálsson. London: Penguin, 1971.

Hrafnkels saga freysgoða. The Icelandic Saga Database. Maintained and edited by Sveinbjorn Thordarson. Accessed June 23, 2023. https://sagadb.org/.

Klaeber, F. R., ed. *Beowulf*. 3rd ed. (with first and second supplements). Lexington: Heath, 1950.

Laws of Early Iceland: Grágás I. Translated by Andrew Dennis, Peter Foote, and Richard Perkins. Winnipeg: University of Manitoba Press, 2007.

Laws of Early Iceland: Grágás II. Translated by Andrew Dennis and Peter Foote. Winnipeg: University of Manitoba Press, 2000.

Laxdæla Saga. Translated by Magnus Magnusson and Hermann Pálsson. New York: Penguin, 1988.

Laxdæla Saga. Íslenzk Fornrit 5. Reykjavík: Hið Íslenzka Fornitafélag, 1934.

Ljósvetninda Saga. Íslenzk Fornrit 10. Reykjavík: Hið Íslenzka Fornitafélag, 1940.

Njal's Saga. Translated by Magnus Magnusson and Hermann Pálsson. New York: Penguin, 1960.

The Prose Edda. Translated by Jesse L. Byock. London: Penguin, 2006.

The Poetic Edda. Translated by Lee M. Hollander. Austin: University of Texas Press, 2001.

"The Saga of the Confederates." In *The Saga of the Icelanders*. Edited by Jane Smiley. Translated by Ruth C. Ellison. New York: Penguin, 2000.

The Saga of Cormac the Skald. Translated by W. G. Collingwood and J. Stefansson. Accessed December 15, 2022, https://sagadb.org/kormaks_saga.en.

The Saga of Gisli the Outlaw. Translated by G. W. Dasent. Accessed March 15, 2022. https://sagadb.org/files/pdf/gisla_saga_surssonar.en.pdf.

The Saga of Grettir the Strong. Translated by Ornólfur Thorsson and Bernard Scudder. New York: Penguin, 2005.

"The Saga of Gunnlaug Serpent-Tongue." In *The Saga of the Icelanders*. Edited by Jane Smiley. Translated by Katrina C. Attwood. New York: Penguin, 2000.

The Saga of Gunnlaugur Snake's Tongue. Translated by E. Paul Durrenberger and Dorothy Durrenberger. Abilene: Associated University Press, 1992.

The Saga of King Hrolf Kraki. Translated by Jesse L. Byock. New York: Penguin, 1998.

"The Saga of the People of Laxardal." *The Saga of the Icelanders*. Edited by Jane Smiley. Translated by Keneva Kunz. New York: Penguin, 2000.

"The Saga of the People of Vatnsdal." *The Saga of the Icelanders*. Edited by Jane Smiley. Translated by Andrew Wawn. New York: Penguin, 2000.

Saxo Grammaticus. *The History of the Danes*. Martlesham: Boydell, 1979.

The Story of the Heath Slayings: Heiðarviga Saga. Translated by William Morris and Eirikr Magnusson. Whitefish: Kessinger, 2010.

Sturluson, Snorri. *The Prose Edda*. Translated by Anthony Faulkes. London: Everyman, 1987.

——. *The Prose Edda*. Translated by Jesse L. Byock. London: Penguin, 2005.

——. *The Prose Edda: Tales from Norse Mythology*. Translated by Jean I. Young. Berkeley: University of California Press, 1966.

Tacitus. *Agricola and Germania*. London: Penguin, 2012.

Thorgilsson, Ari. *The Book of the Icelanders/The Story of the Conversion*. Translated by Siân Grønlie. Viking Society for Northern Research. London: University College London, 2006.

Vatnsdæla Saga. Íslenzk Fornrit 8. Reykjavík: Hið Íslenzka Fornitafélag, 1939.

Vǫðu-Brands Þáttr. Íslenzk Fornrit 10. Reykjavík: Hið Íslenzka Fornitafélag, 1950.

Þorgilsson, Ari. *Íslendingabók*. Edited by Valdimar Ásmundarson. Reykjavik: S. Kristjánsson, 1909. HathiTrust. Accessed Aug. 31, 2023. https://catalog.hathitrust.org/ Record/005734104/Home.

Secondary Sources

Abram, Christopher. "Modeling Religious Experience in Old Norse Conversion Narratives: The Case of Óláfr Tryggvason and Hallfreðr Vandræðaskáld." *Speculum* 90 (2015): 114–57.

Alcoff, Linda. "The Problem of Speaking for Others," *Cultural Critique* 20 (1991–1992): 5–32.

Allen, Judson Boyce. Review of *Rhetoric in the Middle Ages* by James J. Murphy. *Speculum* 52 (1977): 411–14.

Anderson, Sarah M., and Karen Swenson, eds. *Cold Counsel: Women in Old Norse Literature and Mythology*. Oxford: Routledge, 2002.

Andersson, Theodore M. "The King of Iceland." *Speculum* 74 (1999): 923–34.

——. *The Problem of Icelandic Saga Origins: A Historical Survey*. New Haven: Yale University Press, 1964.

Andersson, Theodore M., and William Ian Miller. *Law and Literature in Medieval Iceland: "Ljosvetninga Saga" and "Valla-Ljots Saga."* Palo Alto: Stanford University Press, 1989.

Antonsen, Elmer H. "The Runes: The Earliest Germanic Writing System." In *The Origins of Writing*, edited by Wayne M. Senner, 137–58. Lincoln: University of Nebraska Press, 1989.

Ballif, Michelle, ed. *Theorizing Histories of Rhetoric*. Carbondale: Southern Illinois University Press, 2013.

Barilli, Renato. *Rhetoric*. Translated by Giuliana Menozzi. Minneapolis: University of Minnesota Press, 1989.

Bizzell, Patricia, and Bruce Herzberg. *The Rhetorical Tradition: Readings from Classical Times to the Present*. 2nd ed. Boston: Bedford/St. Martin's, 2001.

Bordieu, Pierre. *Outline of a Theory of Practice*. Cambridge: Cambridge University Press, 1977.

Borrowman, Shane, Robert Lively, and Marcia Kmetz, eds., *Rhetoric in the Rest of the West*. Newcastle upon Tyne: Cambridge Scholars, 2010.

Brownworth, Lars. *The Sea Wolves: A History of the Vikings*. London: Crux, 2014.

Byock, Jesse L. *Feud in the Icelandic Saga*. Berkeley: University of California Press, 1993.

——. "The Icelandic Althing: Dawn of Parliamentary Democracy." In *Heritage and Identity: Shaping the Nations of the North*, ed. J. M. Fladmark, 1–18. Shaftesbury: Donhead, 2002.

——. *Medieval Iceland: Society, Sagas, and Power*. Berkeley: University of California Press, 1988.

——. "Saga Form, Oral Prehistory, and the Icelandic Social Context." *New Literary History* 16 (1984–1985): 153–73.

——. "The Sagas and the Twenty First Century." In *In Honor of Franz Bäuml*, edited by Ursula Schaefer and Edda Spielman, 71–84. Dresden: Dresden University Press, 2001.

——. *Viking Age Iceland*. New York: Penguin, 2001.

——. *Viking Language 1*. Pacific Palisades: Jules, 2013.

——. *Viking Language 2*. Pacific Palisades: Jules, 2015.

Camargo, Martin. "Rhetoric." In *The Seven Liberal Arts in the Middle Ages*, edited by David L. Wagner, 96–124. Bloomington: Indiana University Press, 1983.

Carlquist, Jonas. "The History of Old Nordic Manuscripts III: Old Swedish." In *The Nordic Languages: An International Handbook of the History of the North Germanic Languages*, edited by Oskar Bandle, 808–16. Berlin: Mouton De Gruyter, 2002.

Clark, George. "The Hero and the Theme." In *A Beowulf Handbook*, edited by Robert E. Bjork and John D. Niles, 271–91. Lincoln: University of Nebraska Press, 1998.

Clements, Jonathan. *The Vikings: The Last Pagans or the First Modern Europeans.* Philadelphia: Running, 2005.

Colman, Rebecca V. "Reason and Unreason in Early Medieval Law." *Journal of Interdisciplinary History* 4 (1974): 571–91.

Conley, Thomas M. *Rhetoric in the European Tradition*. Chicago: University of Chicago Press, 1990.

———. "Topics of Vituperation: Some Commonplaces of 4th Century Oratory." In *Philosophia Antiqua, Influences on Peripatetic Rhetoric: Essays in Honor of William W. Fortenbaugh*, edited by David C. Mirhady, 231–38. Leiden: Brill, 2007.

Cooijmans, Christian. *Monarchs and Hydrarchs: The Conceptual Development of Viking Activity Across the Frankish Realm (c. 750–940)*. London: Routledge, 2021.

Crowley, Sharon. "Let Me Get This Straight." In *Writing Histories of Rhetoric*, edited by Victor Vitanza, 128–38. Carbondale: Southern Illinois University Press, 1994.

deCode Genetics. "The Majority of Icelandic Female Settlers Came from the British Isles." deCode Genetics. 2001. Accessed July 27, 2024. www.decode.com/the-majority-of-icelandic-female-settlers-came-from-the-british-isles/.

Driscoll, Matthew J. "Introduction to Manuscript Studies." Lecture given at the Summer School in Scandinavian Manuscript Studies, 12 August 2019. University of Copenhagen.

———. "The Words on the Page: Thoughts on Philology, Old and New." *Creating the Medieval Saga: Versions, Variability and Editorial Interpretations of Old Norse Saga Literature*, edited by Judy Quinn and Emily Lethbridge, 87–104. Odense: University Press of Southern Denmark, 2010.

Dumville, David. *The Churches of Great Britain in the First Viking Age*. Chester: Whithorn, 1997.

Ebenesersdóttir, S. Sunna, et al. "Ancient Genomes from Iceland Reveal the Making of a Human Population." *Science* 360, no. 6392 (June 2018): 1028–32.

Enos, Richard Leo. "The Archaeology of Women in Rhetoric: Rhetorical Sequencing as a Research Method for Historical Studies." *Rhetoric Society Quarterly* 32, no. 1 (Winter 2002): 65–79.

———. "Rhetorical Archaeology: Established Resources, Methodological Tools, and Basic Research Methods." In *The Sage Handbook of Rhetorical Studies*, edited by Andrea Lunsford, 35–52. Newbury Park: Sage, 2009.

———. "Scriptura Etrusca: A Prolegomenon to Roman Rhetoric." In *Rhetoric in the Rest of the West*, edited by Shane Borrowman, Robert Lively, and Marcia Kmetz, 36–61. Newcastle upon Tyne: Cambridge Scholars, 2010.

———. "Theory, Validity and the Historiography of Classical Rhetoric: A Discussion of Archaeological Rhetoric." In *Theorizing Histories of Rhetoric*, edited by Michelle Ballif, 8–24. Carbondale: Southern Illinois University Press, 2013.

Fentress, James, and Chris Wickham. *Social Memory*. Oxford: Blackwell, 1992.

Ferguson, Robert. *The Vikings: A History*. New York: Penguin, 2009.

Fernandez-Garrido, Regla. "Stasis-Theory in Judicial Speeches of Greek Novels." *Greek, Roman, and Byzantine Studies* 49 (2009): 453–72.

Findell, Martin. *Runes*. London: British Museum, 2014.

Foote, P. G. *The Viking Achievement*. London: Sidgwick and Jackson, 1970.

Frederiksen, Britta Olrik. "The History of Old Nordic Manuscripts IV: Old Danish," In *The Nordic Languages: An International Handbook of the History of the North Germanic Languages*, edited by Oskar Bandle, 816–24. Berlin: Mouton De Gruyter, 2002.

Friðriksdottir, Jóhanna Katrín. *Valkyrie: The Women of the Viking World*. London: Bloomsbury, 2020.

———. *Women in Old Norse Literature: Bodies, Words, and Power*. London: Palgrave MacMillan, 2013.

Gabriele, Matthew, and David M. Perry. *The Bright Ages: A New History of Medieval Europe*. New York: Harper Collins, 2021.

Garipzanov, Ildar H., ed. *Conversion and Identity in the Viking Age*. Medieval Identities: Socio Cultural Spaces 5. Turnhout: Brepols, 2014.

Gíslason, Jónas. "Acceptance of Christianity in Iceland in the Year 1000 (999)". *Scripta Instituti Donneriani Aboensis* 13 (1990): 223–55.

Glenn, Cheryl. *Classical Rhetoric Retold: Re-Mapping the Territory*. Abstract. PDF distributed by *ERIC Clearinghouse*, 1993.

———. "Re-Mapping Rhetorical Territory." *Rhetoric Review* 13 (1995): 287–303.

———. *Rhetoric Retold: Regendering the Tradition from Antiquity through the Renaissance*. Carbondale: Southern Illinois University Press, 1997.

Gordon, E.V. *An Introduction to Old Norse*. Oxford: Oxford University Press, 1990.

Grabill, Jeffrey T. *Writing Community Change: Designing Technologies for Citizen Action*. New York: Hampton, 2007.

Graham Campbell, James, and Sean McGrail. *The Viking World*. Reprint Edition. London: Frances Lincoln, 2013.

Gray-Rosendale, Laura, and Sibylle Gruber, eds. *Alternative Rhetorics: Challenges to the Rhetorical Tradition*. New York: SUNY Press, 2001.

Greenblatt, Stephen. *The Swerve*. New York: Norton, 2012.

Gross, Alan G. "Why Hermagoras Still Matters: The Fourth Stasis and Interdisciplinarity." *Rhetoric Review* 23 (2004): 141–55.

Guerra, Valeschka Martins, et al. "The Importance of Honor Concerns Across Eight Countries." *Group Processes and Intergroup Relations* 16 (2012): 298–318.

Gunnlaugsson, Guðvarður Már. "Manuscripts and Palaeography," In *A Companion to Old Norse-Icelandic Literature and Culture*, edited by Rory McTurk, 245–64. Oxford: Blackwell, 2005.

Hastrup, Kirsten. "Cosmography." *Medieval Scandinavia: An Encyclopedia*, edited by Phillip Pulsiano and Kirsten Wolf, 108–9. New York: Garland, 1993.

———. *Culture and History in Medieval Iceland: An Anthropological Analysis of Structure and Change*. Oxford: Oxford University Press, 1985.

———. "Defining A Society: The Icelandic Free State Between Two Worlds." *Scandinavian Studies* 56 (1984): 235–55.

Haugen, Odd Einar. "The Spirit of Lachmann, The Spirit of Bedier: Old Norse Textual Editing in The Electronic Age." Paper presented at the Annual Meeting of the Viking Society, University College London, 2003. Electronic version accessed July 7, 2022. https://bora.uib.no/bora-xmlui/handle/1956/20955.

Hauser, Gerard A. *Introduction to Rhetorical Theory*. 2nd ed. Long Grove: Waveland, 2002.

Hawhee, Deborah, and Christa J. Olson. "Pan-Historiography: The Challenges of Writing History Across Time and Space." In *Theorizing Histories of Rhetoric*, edited by Michelle Ballif, 90–105. Carbondale: Southern Illinois University Press, 2013.

Haywood, John. *North Men: The Viking Saga, AD 793–124*. New York: Thomas Dunne, 2016.

——. *The Penguin Historical Atlas of the Vikings*. New York: Penguin, 1995.

Heath, Malcolm. "The Substructure of Stasis-Theory from Hermagoras to Hermogenes." *The Classical Quarterly* 44 (1994): 114–29.

Heller, Agnes. "Five Approaches to the Phenomenon of Shame." *Social Research* 70 (2003): 1015–30.

Heslop, Kate. *Viking Mediologies: A New History of Skaldic Poetics*. Fordham Series in Medieval Studies. New York: Fordham University Press, 2022.

Hoppmann, Michael J. "A Modern Theory of Stasis." *Philosophy and Rhetoric* 47 (2014): 273–96.

Jakobsson, Armann, and Sverrir Jakobsson. *The Routledge Research Companion to The Medieval Icelandic Sagas*. Oxford: Routledge, 2017.

Jesch, Judith, ed. *The Scandinavians from the Vendel Period to the Tenth Century: An Ethnographic Perspective*. Woodbridge: Boydell, 2012.

——. *The Viking Diaspora*. Oxford: Routledge, 2015.

——. *Women in the Viking Age*. Woodbridge: Boydell, 1991.

Jochens, Jenny. "Late and Peaceful: Iceland's Conversion Through Arbitration in 1000." *Speculum* 74 (1999): 621–55.

——. *Women in Old Norse Society*. Ithaca: Cornell University Press, 1995.

Johnstone, Christopher Lyle, and Richard J. Graff. "Situating Deliberative Rhetoric in Ancient Greece: The Bouleutêrion as a Venue for Oratorical Performance" *Advances in the History of Rhetoric* 21 (2018): 2–88.

Jones, Gwyn. *A History of the Vikings*. Revised ed. Oxford: Oxford University Press, 1984.

Karlsson, Stefán. "The Localisation and Dating of Medieval Icelandic Manuscripts." *Saga-Book* 25 (1998–2001): 138–58. Available at www.medievalists.net/2011/02/the-localisation-and-dating-of-medieval-icelandic-manuscripts/

Kennedy, George. *Aristotle: On Rhetoric*. Oxford: Oxford University Press, 1991.

——. *Classical Rhetoric & Its Christian and Secular Tradition: From Ancient to Modern Times*. 2nd ed. Chapel Hill: University of North Carolina Press, 1999.

——. *Comparative Rhetoric*. Oxford: Oxford University Press, 1998.

——. Review of *Rhetoric in the Middle Ages* by James J. Murphy. *Philosophy and Rhetoric*, 9 (1978): 181–85.

Ker, W. P. *Collected Essays of W.P. Ker*. New York: Macmillan, 1925.

Konstan, David. "Shame in Ancient Greece." *Social Research* 70 (2003): 1031–60.

Larson, Laurence M. *The Earliest Norwegian Laws: Being the Gulathing and the Frostathing Law*. Clark: The Lawbook Exchange, 2011.

——. "Introduction." In *Rhetoric Before and Beyond the Greeks*, 3–31. New York: SUNY Press, 2004.

"Law." *Oxford English Dictionary Online*. Accessed January 23, 2022. https://www.oed.com/.

Lipson, Carol S., and Roberta A. Binkley, eds. *Ancient Non-Greek Rhetorics*. Lauer Series in Rhetoric and Composition. Anderson: Parlor, 2011.

Lively, Robert L. "In Search of Viking Literacy Practices." *Rhetoric Review* 39 1 (2020): 101–17.

——. "'We Must Always Go Fully Armed to Court': The Viking Forensic Tradition." In *Rhetoric in the Rest of the West*, ed. Shane Borrowman, Robert Lively, and Marcia Kmetz, 81–96. Newcastle upon Tyne: Cambridge Scholars, 2010.

Logan, Donald F. *The Vikings in History*. 2nd ed. New York: Harper Collins, 1991.

Lönnroth, Lars. "Rhetorical Persuasion in the Sagas." *Scandinavian Studies* 42 (1970): 157–89.

Lunsford, Andrea A. *Reclaiming Rhetorica: Women In The Rhetorical Tradition*. Pittsburgh: University of Pittsburgh Press, 1995.

Magnusson, Magnus. *Vikings*. Boston: Dutton, 1980.

"The Majority of Icelandic Female Settlers Came from the British Isles." deCode Genetics, 2001. Accessed 14 June 2022. www.decode.com/the-majority-of-icelandic-female-settlers-came-from-the-british-isles/.

Mao, LuMing. "Writing the Other into Histories of Rhetorics: Theorizing the Art of Recontextualization." In *Theorizing Histories of Rhetoric*, ed. Michelle Ballif, 41–57. Carbondale: Southern Illinois University Press, 2013.

Mehler, Natascha. "Þingvellir: A Place of Assembly and a Market?" *Journal of the North Atlantic* 8 (2015): 69–81.

Melnikova, Elena. "How Christian Were Viking Christians?" *Ruthenica* Suppl. 4 (2011): 90–107.

"The Millennium Approaches: 800–900."*National Geographic: Inside the Medieval World*, 67–75. (New York: Time, 2017).

Miller, Joseph M., Michael H. Prosser, and Thomas W. Benson, eds. *Readings in Medieval Rhetoric*. Bloomington: Indiana University Press, 1973.

Miller, Thomas P. "Reinventing Rhetorical Traditions." In *Learning from the Histories of Rhetoric: Essays in Honor of Winifred Bryan Horner*, edited by Theresa Enos, 26–41. Carbondale: Southern Illinois University Press, 1993.

Miller, William Ian. "Avoiding Legal Judgement: The Submission of Disputes to Arbitration in Medieval Iceland." *American Journal of Legal History* 28 (1984): 95–135.

——. *Bloodtaking and Peacemaking*. Chicago: University of Chicago Press, 1990.

——. "Gift, Sale, Payment, Raid: Case Studies in the Negotiation and Classification of Exchange in Medieval Iceland." *Speculum* 61 (1986): 18–50.

——. *Why Is Your Axe Bloody: A Reading of Njal's Saga*. Oxford: Oxford University Press, 2014.

Mommsen, Theodor. *A History of Rome Under the Emperors*. Oxford: Routledge, 1999.

——. "Petrarch's Conception of the 'Dark Ages.'" *Speculum* 17 (1942): 226–42.

Murphy, James J. "Foreword." In *Reclaiming Rhetorica: Women in the Rhetorical Tradition*, edited by Andrea A. Lunsford, ix–xi. Pittsburgh: University of Pittsburgh Press, 1995.

——. *Rhetoric in the Middle Ages: A History of Rhetorical Theory from Saint Augustine to the Renaissance.* Berkeley: University of California Press, 1974.

——. ed. *A Short History of Writing Instruction.* 3rd ed. Oxford: Routledge, 2012.

Nagy, Gregory. "The Library of Pergamon as a Classical Model." In *Pergamon: Citadel of the Gods.* Harvard Theological Studies 46, edited by H. Koester, 185–232. Cambridge, MA: University of Harvard Press, 1998.

National Museet (Copenhagen), "The Transition to Christianity." *National Museet.* Accessed June 21, 2022. https://en.natmus.dk/historical-knowledge/denmark/prehistoric-period-until-1050-ad/the-viking-age/religion-magic-death-and-rituals/the-transition-to-christianity/.

Norton-Smith, John. Review of *Rhetoric in the Middle Ages* by James J. Murphy. *Medium Aevum* 47 (1978): 326–27.

Oskarsson, Thorir. "Rhetoric and Style." In *A Companion to Old Norse-Icelandic Literature and Culture*, edited by Rory McTurk, 354–71. Oxford: Blackwell, 2005.

Owen, Olwyn, ed. *Things in the Viking World.* Reykjavík: Shetland Amenity Trust, 2012.

Page, R. I. *Chronicles of the Vikings.* London: The British Museum, 1995.

Pernot, Lauren. *Epideictic Rhetoric: Questioning the Stakes of Ancient Praise.* Austin: University of Texas Press, 2015.

——. *Rhetoric in Antiquity.* Translated by W.E. Higgins. Washington, DC: The Catholic University of America Press, 2005.

Price, Neil. *Children of Ash and Elm.* New York: Basic, 2020.

Pringle, Heather. "New Visions of the Vikings." *National Geographic* 231, no. 3 (2017): 30–51.

Reinsma, Luke. "Rhetoric in England: The Age of Ælfric, 970–1020" *Communication Monographs* 44 (1977): 390–403.

Riisoy, Anne Irene. "Performing Oaths in Eddic Poetry: Viking Age Fact or Medieval Fiction." *Journal of the North Atlantic* Special 8 (2016): 141–56.

Rindal, Magnus. "The History of Old Nordic Manuscripts II: Old Norwegian (incl. Faroese)," In *The Nordic Languages: An International Handbook of the History of the North Germanic Languages*, edited by Oskar Bandle, 801–8. Berlin: Mouton De Gruyter, 2002.

Roesdahl, Else. *The Vikings.* New York: Penguin, 1998.

Roesdahl, Else, and David M. Wilson, eds. *From Viking to Crusader: Scandinavia and Europe 800–1200.* Milan: Rizzoli, 1992.

Ross, Margaret Clunies. *The Cambridge Introduction to The Old Norse-Icelandic Sagas.* Cambridge: Cambridge University Press, 2010.

——. *A History of Old Norse Poetry and Poetics.* Woodbridge: Brewer, 2005.

Sanmark, Alexandra. "The Case of the Greenlandic Assembly Sites." *Journal of the North Atlantic*, Special Volume 2 (2009): 178–92.

——. *Power and Conversion—A Comparative Study of Christianization in Scandinavia.* Occasional Papers in Archaeology 34. Uppsala: Uppsala University Press, 2004.

——. *Viking Law and Order: Places and Rituals of Assembly in the Medieval North.* Edinburgh: Edinburgh University Press, 2017.

Sawyer, Peter. *The Oxford Illustrated History of the Vikings.* Oxford: Oxford University Press, 2001.

Scheel, Roland. "Introduction." In *Narrating Law and Laws of Narration*. Berlin: De Gruyter, 2020.

Schön, Ebbe. *Asa-Tors Hammare, Gudar Och Jättar i Tro Och tradition*. Värnamo: Fält & Hässler, 2004.

Sheard, Cynthia Miecznikowski. "The Public Value of Epideictic Rhetoric." *College English* 58 (1996): 765–94.

Short, William R. *Icelanders in the Viking Age*. Jefferson: McFarland, 2010.

Shweder, Richard A. "Toward a Deep Cultural Psychology of Shame." *Social Research* 70 (2003): 1109–30.

Sigurðsson, Gísli. *The Medieval Icelandic Saga and Oral Tradition: A Discourse on Method*. Washington, DC: Center for Hellenic Studies, 2004.

Sigurðsson, Jón Viðar. *Viking Friendship: The Social Bond in Iceland and Norway, c. 900–1300*. Ithaca: Cornell University Press, 2017.

Smith, Adam. "The Limitations of Doxa: Agency and Subjectivity from an Archaeological Point of View." *Journal of Social Archaeology*, 1 (2001): 155–71.

Somerville, Angus A., and R. Andrew McDonald. *The Vikings and Their Age*. Companions to Medieval Studies Series. Toronto: University of Toronto Press, 2013.

Sørensen, Preben Meulengracht. *The Unmanly Man: Concepts of Sexual Defamation in Early Northern Society*. Translated by Joan Turville-Petre. Odense: University of Southern Denmark Press, 1983.

Stern, Charlotte. Review of *Rhetoric in the Middle Ages* by James J. Murphy. *Romance Philology* 30 (1977): 663–65.

Straumsheim, Carl Frederik Schou. "Peacemaking in the Middle Ages." The Centre for Advanced Study (CAS). Partner.sciencenorway.no. Accessed June 16, 2024. https://partner.sciencenorway.no/cas-centre-for-advanced-study-forskningno-history/peacemaking-in-the-middle-ages/1455092.

Strecker, Ivo, and Stephen Tyler. *Culture and Rhetoric*. Oxford: Berghahn, 2012.

Svensson, Lars. "Palaeography," In *Medieval Scandinavia: An Encyclopedia*, edited by Phillip Pulsiano, 491–96. London: Routledge, 1993.

Tómasson, Sverrir. "The History of Old Nordic Manuscripts I: Old Icelandic." In *The Nordic Languages: An International Handbook of the History of the North Germanic Languages*, edited by Oskar Bandle, 793–801. Berlin: Mouton De Gruyter, 2002.

Van Deusen, Natalie M. "Sworn Sisterhood? On the (Near-)Absence of Female Friendship from the *Íslendingasǫgur*," *Scandinavian Studies* 86 (2014): 52–71.

Vardoulakis, Dimitris. "Stasis: Notes Towards Agonist Democracy." *Theory and Event*, 20 (2017): 699–725.

Vickers, Brian. *In Defence of Rhetoric*. Oxford: Clarendon, 1988.

Walker, Jeffrey. *The Genuine Teachers of This Art*. Columbia: University of South Carolina Press, 2011.

——. *Rhetoric and Poetics in Antiquity*. Oxford: Oxford University Press, 2000.

Wegner-Trayner, Etienne and Beverly Wegner-Trayner. *Introduction to Communities of Practice: A Brief Overview of the Concept and Its Uses*. WordPress, 2015. Accessed August 30, 2022. https://wenger-trayner.com/introduction-to-communities-of-practice/.

White, Hayden. "Historicism, History, and the Figurative Imagination." *History and Theory* 14, no. 4 (1975): 48–67.

White, James Boyd. "Reading Law and Reading Literature: Law as Language." In *Heracles' Bow: Essays on the Rhetoric and Poetics of the Law*, 77–106. University of Wisconsin Press, 1985.

——. "Rhetoric and Law: The Arts of Cultural and Communal Life." In *Heracles' Bow: Essays on the Rhetoric and Poetics of the Law*, 28–48. Madison: University of Wisconsin Press, 1985.

Williams, Gareth, Peter Pentz, and Matthias Wemhoff, eds. *Vikings: Life and Legends*. Ithaca: Cornell University Press, 2014.

Winroth, Anders. *The Age of the Vikings*. Princeton: Princeton University Press, 2014.

——. *The Conversion of Scandinavia: Vikings, Merchants, and Missionaries in the Remaking of Northern Europe*. New Haven: Yale University Press, 2012.

Wolf, Kirsten. *Viking Age: Everyday Life During the Extraordinary Era of the Norsemen*. New York: Sterling, 2013.

Woods, Marjorie Curry. *Classroom Commentaries: Teaching the Poetria Nova across Medieval and Renaissance Europe*. Columbus: Ohio State University Press, 2010.

"A World Divided: 800–900." *Inside the Medieval World*, 57–65. National Geographic Books. New York: Time, 2017.

INDEX

Printed and bound by CPI Group (UK) Ltd, Croydon, CR0 4YY

02/12/2024

14603653-0001